Reflections

*Prizewinning Poetry, Essays,
and Short Stories*

from the

*Seventh Annual Roane County
Student Writing Contest
Anthology
2015-2016*

*Edited by
Roane Writers Group*

REFLECTIONS Copyright © 2016 by the Roane Writers Group.
All rights reserved.
Manufactured in the United States of America.

For information, write:

The Roane Writers Group
1004 Bradford Way
Kingston, TN 37763

Cover design: Kat Moore

ISBN 13: 978-1532862670

Dedication

To the Cliff Lynch Family.

Contents

Introduction by B.J. Gillum i

In Memoria iii

The Winners

High School Short Story
    Grand Prize Winner – Emily Boswell, Orion 1
    First Place – Veronica Ross, How to Save a Life 8
    Second Place – Reves Shaefer, Six Years for One Night 15
    Third Place – Hanah May, Prospero Raven 19
    Founder's Choice Award - Aaron Walton, Monster 23

Middle School Short Story
    First Place – Lillian Bacon, Bad Times 32
    Second Place – Rebekah Brooks, The Agent 36
    Third Place – Madi Thompson, Why I'm No Longer a Babysitter 39

Elementary School Short Story
    First Place – Abigail Mynatt, Escaping a Concentration Camp 41
    Second Place – Layla Vowell, Joe Joe and the Bees 44
    Third Place – Allbree Hanshaw, The Dummy 47
    A. Nonnie Muss Award – Luke Gunter, The Gate 49

High School Poetry
    First Place – Abby Jackson, Education 54
    Second Place – Kylie Richardson, Imperfect Scars 56
    Third Place – Mari Claire Crass, Big Brother 58
    Fourth Place – Matthew Webb, The Right Track 61

Middle School Poetry
    First Place – Sydney Bryant, Kids of Divorce 63
    Second Place – Emily Scott, Little Demon 65
    Third Place – Anna Fink, Tonight 67

Elementary School Poetry
    First Place – Loretta Ketterer, My Map of Peace 69
    Second Place – Caiydend Grigsby, One Spring Day 71
    Third Place – Evan Chen, Spring is Here 73

High School Essay
    First Place – Adrianna Hicks, Dress Code 74
    Second Place – Emma Jackson, Freedom to be Me 76

Middle School Essay
    First Place – Blake Parks, Learning Foreign Languages 78
    Second Place – Savanna Longmire, Cell Phone Usage at School 82
    Third Place – Amy Sellers, Equal Rights 86

Best of the Rest

High School Short Story
    Reagan Conley, Hacked 91
    Joseph Frost, My True Best Friend 97
    Emma Jackson, The Never Ending Love 101
    Kelvey Nabors, The Girl with Purple Hair 105

Middle School Short Story
    Mia Janikula, The House 109

Elementary School Short Story
    Kiyah Love, The Dog and the Owl 111
    Bricen Mee, The Candy War 113

High School Poetry
    Ethan Burnett, A Strife with the Unknown 115
    Kelvey Nabors, The Boy with the Thunderstorm Voice 117
    Reves Schaefer, Sisters 119

Kallie Sohm, Lost in the Pages 121

Middle School Poetry
    Dalton Bacon, Names 123
    Jacob Gardner, Gym Class 124
    Aubrey Walden, Leap of Leopards 125

Middle School Essay
    Marlena Alexander, The Death of Edgar Allan Poe 127
    Taylor Bonafede, Social Media 130
    Rebekah Brooks, The Wonderful World of Lucid
    Dreaming 133
    Sarah Collins, Child Abuse and Adoption 136
    Lucas Goldschmidt, The Importance of Music 139
    Dequin Kile, Chris Kyle 141
    April Lance, Scotty McCreery 147
    Kadi Lewis, Print and Pixels: A Guide to Books 150
    Alex Limburg, Service Dog Benefits 154
    Alysan Limburg, Siberian Husky 158
    Cheyenne Pine, Self-Harm 161
    Ben Poczobut, The History of Lacrosse 164
    Connor Quigley, Football 167
    Savannah Rayburn, Animal Cruelty 170
    Emilee Schaefer, A Man's Best Friend 174
    Stephen Wishnia, Is your faith under attack? 177

Acknowledgements 181

What can I do to help? 183

Special Thanks to Our Supporting Advertisers 185

Introduction

I have heard more than two hundred thousand books are written and published every year in this country. So it is logical that you might ask, "Why another anthology?" We had a slow start seven years ago when only a few entries were received and the Grand Prize was a fifty dollar US Savings Bond. The Roane County Student Writing Contest grew yearly and received support from school teachers and administrators as well as Roane County officials.

An Arts Builds Communities grant from the Tennessee Arts Commission shared the cost of publication while the generosity of fellow Roane Countians provided the means to give cash prizes and one large Scholarship to contest winners. Roane State Community College donated the use of the O'Brien Theater for the Awards Program. Volunteers judged and scored the entries, compiled the entries into a manuscript, created cover art, and coordinated with the publisher. Dozens of volunteers are involved at some level throughout this process. This Anthology is the final tangible product of that effort.

This anthology reflects the effort of the students who entered and won a place in a published work – they are now Published Authors! That fact engenders pride in their accomplishment. We hope it will also inspire them to see writing in a new light: not as labor or work or a classroom assignment, but as a way to express their individual artistic creativity. Too, they can take pride in contributing to a creation larger than themselves. This anthology provides its authors with recognition, inspiration and pride in a job well done. The Roane Writers Group congratulates the winners and 'Best of the Rest' and all others who participated in this project.

BJ Gillum, President

Roane Writers Group

In Memoria

This year, a member of the Roane Writers Group lost one of its members. We would like to honor her memory in this edition of the Student Anthology.

Suzyn Marie Chandler

Born August 1st 1967 Died January 9th 2016

Suzyn was a living walking miracle. I have epilepsy and the doctors told me to stop taking my medicine while I was pregnant. I regained consciousness at least six times at the bottom of the stairs; I also fell off the second story balcony when I was about eight months pregnant. She stayed with me to term.

At the age of ten, the bones in her left hip died. The doctors told her she would probably never walk again. Eight operations, a fused hip, and four years in a hospital, but she proved them wrong.

When she started college, we found out she had Asperger's Syndrome and Cerebral Palsy. Again it did not stop her. She took off like a rocket and graduated with honors and a 3.5 grade point average. She was also a published author.

When she was 12, the doctor told me if she lived to be 35, I would be very lucky; she died at the age of 48. I had her for 13 years longer than the doctors would ever have dreamed possible.

I had never seen much love in my life. I thought I was broken, that I could not love; then Suzyn stepped in and showed me I could love and the twenty years we have been together is the biggest blessing of my life.

I will love her and miss her always.

- Stefanie Chandler

High School Short Story
GRAND PRIZE WINNER

Emily Boswell is a twelfth grade student at Roane County High School.

When I'm not stalking my customers in the produce department of Kroger, I'm either watering my succulent collection or listening to a stranger pour out their life story to my ever- hungry ears. Between the trials of work and school, I'm usually dabbling in the arts, dancing around on city sidewalks, or creating worlds through the written word.

Animals have a special part in my life. I've always been fascinated by all the different species and yearn to gain more knowledge about them. Once I'm able, I hope to have a farm someday where I can be surrounded by all sorts of nature and pursue my art.

I first started writing for fun when I was in middle school, I started making up characters with my best friend in New Jersey. I've thus far created 60+ characters, all with separate detailed backgrounds and interests. I found pleasure in writing about my various characters, building their obstacles and orchestrating their triumphs.

Orion, the main character featured in the following story, came from my love of the octopus, the alienation I felt around my peers, and the sense of confusion the world gave me as a young one.

Orion

The air was heavy and warm. The air wasn't air but a clear liquid that only made its matter known by the slow moving bubbles that passed through its slippery conglomerate of atoms to reach the air bubble that had been caught at the top. The water gently poured into the space on and around yellow irises. Those eyes glided lazily around the world presented before him.

This world was warped by the cylinder of glass that surrounded his floating body, painting the world into strange blobs of color and texture. A blue hand rested on the thick glass that contained its owner. The pads of blue fingers slid down the surface of the smooth glass, taking in its texture, which would be the first texture the hand would ever feel, besides the gliding caress of the surrounding liquid.

A movement caught the yellow eyes, and they snapped to the source. A metal hand-like appendage about two feet in length emerged from a panel at the top of the cylinder above his head and slowly descended the length of his body, dragging a red laser grid over the peaks and valleys of his humanesque form. This was the first time he saw himself. He could only assume he was a he, for there were no markers of human gender depicted on his lower body. The gentle voice of knowledge in his head supplied this language of letters he had never before thought in, yet described his world to him.

Before this language, there had only been number codes that defined the existence of the world around him. His body was no longer a system of 1s and 0s but now legs and arms, flesh and skeleton. There were now colors, filters of light that left a single brilliance in an object and defined it from the surrounding backdrop of other colors and shapes. His reality was now like that of a person, not that of a computer. His programming was his guide through this new exciting world of vision and would soon help lead him through the other four senses as they developed. But first had come vision, filling the rods and cones of his artificially constructed eyeballs.

Next came touch, though he had already begun his understanding of touch when his fingertips dragged down the surface of the smooth glass, but now he was truly exploring it. His other hand pressed against the glass and his mind supplied an action.

Push, it murmured gently in the caverns of his mind. Orion obeyed and began to apply a gentle pressure against the hard surface; it groaned under his power but did not change.

More, came the voice, and again he listened. This time, he applied a greater force until cracks spider-webbed through the surface of the glass, and now compromised, it shattered under his hands. It clinked to the tile floor below, allowing the liquid that had surrounded his body to run forth from the shattered glass and spill all over. His ears rang as the liquid sprang forth from them too and revealed another sense he would soon learn more of. The gift of Sound.

Somewhere in Orion's chest, two shriveled pieces of flesh screamed to be filled. Pain shot from them and sang in Orion's nerves. His eyes widened, and he opened his mouth as if to scream but could not, nor knew how to do it. The voice whispered softly to him.

Breathe.

The command was very foreign to Orion's mind, but his body knew what to do. His mouth opened once more, and his chest compressed, causing the faintly blue liquid to be expelled from his lungs and spill from his parted lips. Contently empty, his chest expanded, pulling air into the shriveled sacs in it. Then the process repeated until the pain was no longer a shooting, stinging scream but a dull, throbbing ache. Orion had learned about something new. Pain.

Orion felt the last of the water trickle away. He moved forward, taking one step and placing his left foot in a puddle of blue liquid and glass. There were little songs of pain, but he ignored their melody to continue forward with the next foot until he was standing in the center of the large, white room. Bland walls and cold tile floors met his eyes, and a new silence met his ears. This silence had an air of possibility to it, as if at any moment, it could be broken with some sort of vibrational energy. It was an exciting silence, not like the impossible, imposed silence his old nonfunctional ears had been accustomed to.

He could hear soft beeps and the whirring of machines as he stepped further from his cylindrical home to the wider expanse of the room. He scanned its features, noticing more than simple colors and shapes as his eyes adjusted. Hulking masses of machinery, wires, and light lurked in the corners and against the walls of the stark white room. As he looked around, he noticed a stray beam of glittering light making a little spotlight on the floor.

He walked over slow and easy, moving each part of himself like it was alien until he reached the light. His hand raised in a fluid motion to the light, and it danced around the textures of his skin. It amazed him. His lips and corresponding cheeks twitched and lightly spasmed into a movement new to him and universal to others. A smile. The voice in his head chuckled softly.

If this is so amazing to you, I can't imagine what you'll think of the city. Now c'mon.

Orion's eyes followed the ray's length to where it snuck in through a high window. Due to Orion's staggering seven-foot form, it was no issue to reach onto the frame, but it took him a few extra moments to haul himself up and out of it, barely wriggling his large form out of the window's narrow width. He fell into a shower of sunlight, the warm rays casting his skin in its golden glow. All four of his eyes blinked separately to adjust themselves to the new world's sensations. He basked in the sunlight, a feeling of deja vu washing over him. Memories of picnics and barbeques, of beach trips and sunburns, of a little girl splashing in the salty waves, of himself diving into the cooling blue water. Then he heard a quiet laugh ring in his brain.

Those are mine, big blue, so don't feel bad about not understanding them, spoke the voice in a bittersweet tone as Orion pressed on into the surrounding ring of trees. His feet padded against the lush moss and crunchy pine needles of the underbrush. His eyes scanned the horizon dotted with green leaves and striped with ruddy-brown tree trunks until dots of light became evident over the horizon.

It looked like the setting sun had leaked onto the greenery and set it ablaze with brilliant light. His eyebrows pulled together, and his eyes narrowed as his mind searched for an answer from his own memories, but those were short, watercolor movies in his head that made little sense. Another department of his brain was much more helpful. The voice's, Jamie's, memories offered up an image: collections of tall glass structures swarmed by busy humans that scurried about between them. The smells of warm food, smoke, gas, and metal filled his nose as the sounds of electric car horns and whirrs rang in his ears. This place seemed unpleasant to Orion. It seemed like too much all at once.

It's not so bad, blue, but I think it's best if we wait awhile. It's been a long first day. How about we rest first?

Orion agreed and found a place to rest in a patch of soft grass within the swaying arms of a weeping willow. He eased to his knees and lay down slowly, as if testing the earth to see if it would allow him there. It gave no protest as his head rested among the bending blades of grass.

Orion's lungs filled with sweet, fresh air before he exhaled a long sigh through his nose. The sigh seemed to release the tension in his body. His limbs lay sprawled out around him in a lazy, languid sort of way. The sun fell from its throne to give way for the moon's nightly reign. Crickets and insects sang in the night as nature's lullaby to the welcome stranger that lay in its grasp. A feeling of heaviness rested in Orion's eyes and he succumbed to it. Silent, stretched out in nature's loving caress, Orion allowed himself to fall into the slowly churning waves of a restful sleep.

High School Short Story
FIRST PLACE

Veronica Ross is a twelfth grade student at Roane County High School.

How to Save a Life

"Evie it's okay. We'll figure this out."

"Duke, I'm not even sure I know what to figure out."

It's November 22, 1963. I'm 17 years old. I walk home from my job at the local hospital with Duke, my best friend. Whatever our souls are made of, his and mine are the same. Sometimes I think I'm in love with him. Sometimes I think he's just my best friend. Today, he is my rock.

As I was preparing to leave work, a dying man was wheeled in on a stretcher. As he rolled past, I was consumed by an indescribable feeling. I knew without a shadow of a doubt that he would be dead soon. One could call it intuition, but I know intuition, and that's not what this felt like. This was like a prediction, like I was sensing the future.

Duke and I arrive at my house. He grabs my shoulders and assures me once more, "It's going to be okay. Let's go inside, watch your man on television, and let this settle."

I open the door, and my mom screams, "Evie! It's starting! The president is entering downtown!"

I slide in beside her and she thrusts a bowl of popcorn onto my lap. One could say that Mom and I are obsessed with Jack Kennedy. They couldn't be more right. He's a little old for me and a little young for my mom, and he might be married. But has any of that ever stopped him before?

Mom turns up the volume, and the three of us settle in to watch Jack cruise down the streets of Dallas. "Oh look at Jackie! That pink suit is just adorable!" Mom exclaims.

"Jackie?" I scoff. "Look at Jack. He's looking as handsome as ever."

All of a sudden, my stomach drops and my breath catches in my throat. For the second time today, I know someone is about to die. I can feel the certainty from my head to my toes.

"He's going to die," I repeat monotonously to my mother.

"Well, of course he is," she says with a roll of her eyes.

Jack's car starts to round a corner. "No," I mutter, "he's going to die right now."

My mom looks at me incredulously. A shot rings out. And then another. Jack's brains are in his lap; Jackie is fleeing for her life. My mom screams. I can't move.

Duke looks at me with uncertainty in his eyes. I slowly nod my head. *Another predicted death.* Before my mom realizes what I've done, Duke leads me from the room.

"Duke," I begin to cry, "what am I going to do? I can't handle this. I don't want whatever this is! This isn't the kind of superpower anyone dreams of!"

Duke paces for a few minutes, then he sighs. "We're going to do all we can do. You'll have to quit your job at the hospital. There's too much death there. Then, after we graduate, I'll get us jobs far, far away from death. That's all I can do."

I don't know that I have faith in his plan. I feel sick, and my head reels, but I nod. I lay my head down in his lap, and I fall asleep.

I resigned from the hospital three days later. Soon after, President Kennedy was put to rest. The world has moved on now, and so have I. I've attributed my experiences to a disruption in the force and nothing more. It's been four years now, and I haven't predicted a single death.

Duke stuck to his plan and managed to get the two of us jobs in the kitchen at the glamorous Ambassador Hotel in Los Angeles, California. Today is June 5, 1968, and tonight Bobby Kennedy will speak at the hotel.

"A Kennedy!" my mother squealed when I told her. "Evie, this is your dream come true!" And it would be ... had I not predicted his brother's assassination five years ago.

Regardless, I expect this to be an experience I'll never forget. Toward the end of my shift, security enters and surrounds the kitchen. Duke mouths to me from across the room, "He's coming through here!!"

All of a sudden, there stands Bobby Kennedy. As my co-worker Juan steps forward to shake Bobby's hand, my stomach clenches and that long-absent feeling grasps me again. I don't hesitate this time. "He's going to die! Someone help him!"

There's a moment of complete silence. In slow motion, everyone turns to look at me. Everyone except for Duke, who dives for Bobby. A shot rings out. Then I feel something connect with my head and the world fades away.

I come to in a creaky bed in a cold, drab room. Duke sits in a chair facing the door. When I stir, he looks over and smiles. "Did you hit your head when you were falling for me?"

I smirk at him, but I say nothing. My memory is fuzzy, so I actually don't remember much of what happened to me. Duke frowns. "You don't remember, do you?" he asks.

I shake my head. He recounts the night, the assassination. I interrupt, "Wait ... you didn't say attempted assassination. So Bobby really did die then?"

Duke nods solemnly, wringing his hands suspiciously. "What?" I demand forcefully.

"Well," he starts, "of course the authorities realize you aren't the assassin. They caught him: Sirhan B. Sirhan." He laughs at the name and then pauses.

"But?" I encourage.

"But," he continues, "they can't let a talent like yours go to waste."

I stare at him. "Duke…"

"Evie, you're going to have to work for them. You'll be like honorary secret service. You'll monitor the president at all times, and you'll alert anyone if you sense danger."

"But, Duke, I only know a split second before it happens!"

He rubs my hand and sighs, "Yes, but a split second could save a life."

Today a split second will save a life. It's March 30, 1981, twenty-two years later. Today I'm escorting Ronald Reagan from a speaking engagement at the Washington Hilton Hotel. After the event concludes, the president approaches the exit.

"Ms. O'Brien," the President says with a smile.

"Mr. President." I nod in acknowledgment as I fall into stride with Jerry Parr, the *"Special Agent in Charge."* We exit the building, and the president shakes hands and kisses babies. As we near a roped off section of bystanders, I'm overwhelmed by a familiar feeling. I grab Parr's arm.

"He's about to die!" I scream in his ear. Parr jumps into action. Shots ring out. The Press Secretary is shot down, and a cop follows behind him. Parr shoves Reagan into the car, and I am frozen still.

"O'Brien!" someone yells from the motorcade. I turn and run to the car. As the door closes I'm allowed a few moments of celebration.

But the celebration is not long lived. When I arrive home I'm informed that the President was indeed shot, and he is currently in surgery. Currently on his deathbed, for all I know. The next several hours pass in slow motion. I've had this job for thirteen years, and I've never had anything happen, but today, when I was actually needed, I failed.

I'm wallowing in my guilt when the phone rings. "Hello?" I answer.

"Hey, Evie. It's Duke."

"Duke?" I ask cautiously. "Why are you calling?"

"Have you seen the news?" he asks. My stomach sinks. He takes my silence as an answer. "The President is going to be fine. He should be back on the job within a month. I'm betting that's because of you."

My sobs of relief are my only response. Duke waits until I'm composed. "A split second saved a life today, my love."

"That brings us to today: 2016, 35 years later. I'm seventy years old and no longer able to keep up with Washington. It's finally time for me to retire. I would like to think my best friends from over the years: Misters Johnson, Nixon, Ford, Carter, Reagan, H.W. Bush, Clinton, W. Bush, and to my current best friend, Mr. Obama. These nine men have provided me with an abundance of unforgettable experiences. I am forever grateful.

At seventeen, I never imagined my life would end up like this. But after forty-eight years on the job, I can say I wouldn't have had it any other way. Thank you."

Everyone begins to cheer. Even though the room is crowded, my eyes still connect with the ones that know me best. Duke rises slowly, tears in his eyes. He holds up his hand and blows me a kiss. My heart settles into my chest because I know my life isn't over yet.

I still have many years to spend with my oldest best friend – my true best friend.

High School Short Story
SECOND PLACE

Reves Shaefer is a ninth grade student who is home-schooled.

Six Years for One Night

Hello, my name is Rod, and I'd like to share a story with you that I don't tell many people. It took place on a cold, dark Thursday night.

"See you Monday, Mr. Peters!" I shouted as I sauntered out of the dojo. Studying the martial arts of Jiu Jitsu and the rare Isshinryu Karate, I was perfecting my skills under the guidance of Mr. Peters. I started training when I was eleven, and after six years I held the rank of a 2nd degree black belt in karate and a purple belt in jiu jitsu.

The night seemed like any other as I road home with my friend, Dean. We made our usual stop by the local Taco Bell, and Dean dropped me off at my house.

"Talk to you next week, man," I remarked as I grabbed my duffle bag. As I approached the front porch, my mom, Diane, flicked the light on for me and unlocked the door.

"How was karate tonight?" Diane inquired. Before I could answer, she added, "Oh! Don't forget your short story assignment is due tomorrow."

"Yes, I remember, Mom, but thanks for reminding me how much I procrastinate," I joked. "Where are Marie and Jane?" I queried.

"Those two are downstairs watching a movie," Mom answered.

Out of habit, I lazily flung my duffle bag on the floor and headed to my room. After changing clothes, I ambled to the kitchen seeking to fill my never ending appetite. As I nonchalantly strolled down the hallway, I suddenly halted to a stop, hearing an alarming sound. It sounded like someone was kicking the door downstairs. Before I had time to comprehend the situation, the door burst open, and both of my sisters started screaming.

"Shut up and get on the ground, or I'll shoot!" a man yelled.

"I'll find the mom!" rumbled another voice.

Immediately, thoughts flashed through my mind like bullets. "Are they going to kill my sisters? What do they want? What will they do to us? I need to call 911. Where is Mom?"

Quickly yet quietly I ran to my parents' room and grabbed my bewildered mother. "Did you hear that, Rod?" Mom frantically questioned, only to be hushed.

"Be quiet," I insisted as I pulled her into the walk-in closet. Right as I closed the closet door I heard one of the intruders prowling down the hallway. "Mom, I need you to call 911," I whispered as I sat her down in a corner and covered her with clothes. Seconds later the man entered the bedroom.

Being as quiet as possible, I heard the man cock his gun. After a few excruciatingly long seconds of silence the door burst open! There stood a tower of a man with a .44 magnum pistol.

Before I could even think, my reflexes allowed me to step out of the way right as the gun fired. With ears ringing vibrantly and feeling like I was in a bad dream, I heard the seemingly distant scream of my mother behind me. As if in slow motion, I used the self-defense technique I had practiced so many times. With explosion I struck the criminal's wrist with one hand and grabbed the gun with the other. With adrenaline pumping, I swiped the gun right out of the man's grasp, while the man clutched his hand in pain!

"Put your hands behind your head and get on the ground!" I demanded authoritatively as if I were a police officer. The huge man slunk to the floor as if he had lost his spine.

"Mom, take this gun; if he tries to get up, you'll know what to do," I explained to my trembling mom.

Not wasting a second, I headed down the hallway only to meet another angry thug. The man opened fire, blowing a round through my shoulder. Entering the fight-flight-freeze response and not even acknowledging the wound, I tackled the man to the ground.

The gun skidded across the floor in the middle of the scuffle, and I went to pounding away on my grounded attacker! Using every technique I had been taught, I dominated my opponent, until the man grabbed something from his pocket. It was a knife! Taking a deep slice to the stomach, I was thrown across the floor.

With the gunshot wound and the abdominal cut taking their toll, I staggered to my feet only to be pushed back down. The man swiftly jumped on top of me! Blow after blow landed on my swollen, numb face. The man grabbed my hair and reached for his knife. As he lifted his blade to end my young life, two gunshots rang throughout the house!

The giant of a man fell limp on the floor nearly dead, and behind him stood a shaky Marie holding a smoking revolver. Marie ran over to assist me. Still in survival mode, I asked in a raspy voice, "Are there any more?"

"There were only two of them," Marie softly answered.

With concern in my voice I stuttered, "Mom ... Mom is in the bedroom with the other man. She needs help!"

Marie whispered, "I'm going to help Mom; we're going to be okay, Rod." Breathing a sigh of relief, I rested my head on the floor.

After the police and ambulance arrived, I was taken to the hospital for emergency surgery where they saved my life. The wounded criminal was also rushed to emergency surgery and recovered, only to face a long sentence in prison with his partner in crime. Both of the criminals were sentenced to prison for a class B felony. I never would have guessed that those six years of continual training weren't merely for tournaments or sport. All of the repetitive motion and self-defense drills were for one night and had one purpose – to protect my family. I had trained six years for one night.

High School Short Story
THIRD PLACE

Hanah May is a tenth grade student at Oliver Springs High School.

Prospero Raven

My precious dear Annabel Lee, it has been, what, oh, some four months ever since you have left from this earth and joined the angels in heaven. Your tomb lies beneath the dense mossy seaside grass. I come to visit you every day, and I sit beside your sepulcher and have timeless conversations with you. You never respond, but I know you're listening to me. Times goes by slower and slower each day, my love for you has grown stronger as each day passes.

As I sit in this empty house we built, I ponder on the many conversations and adventures we had together. Oh Annabel, do you remember when we were young? I miss sneaking in through your window at the darkest of nights. I miss just looking at each other and adoring every perfection and flaw. I miss watching your eyes light up like the north star when I spoke about our plans for the future. Annabel, you are everything I have ever wanted. We built this very house together and right before we could decorate the inside, the angels sent a chilling wind to take your soul. This house is not only empty but heartless. All the love and compassion we shared in this house left with you, my dear Annabel.

I have thought out many ways to contact you, but not one of them seem to work. Everyone takes me as a madman. They label me as the dark widowed poet who lost his wife. Many people have spread rumors saying that I killed you, my sweet Annabel. I have not yet gone into town ever since you left me. I keep a quiet, still life, cooped up in a cold, dark, heartless house. A young boy comes to my house to ask me questions about writing; he is planning on being journalist for the town. He seems to at least fifteen. Intelligence speaks within his cobalt pastel eyes, his hair complemented his fair complexion.

This young boy's name is Prospero Raven, but he tells me to call him Pro for short. Pro tells me that the town speaks of me as the dark, eerie, mysterious widowed poet, who holds himself captive in a lonely house. Pro comes to me and asks about my writing style and how I come up with these miraculous and marvelous stories. I sort of chuckled and smiled and said, "My mind is a monster that tells stories of his wildest dreams and I write them down. You see, my life hasn't been easy. Annabel was my darling, and my love and compassion for her could have stretched as far as the east is from the west."

But anyway, Pro began to tell me he wanted to start visiting me more so he could absorb as much information as he could about writing. I told him to come by anytime he wanted to.

Time passed, it has been nor one, nor two, but three weeks since Prospero Raven has visited me. My sweet Annabel, as I lay by your sarcophagus I begin to think. What in heaven's sake is going on? Have the angels murdered poor Prospero's soul; did the angels send a chilling wind to murder him too? No, that cannot be the case, I will not accept it. Is was nightfall. I shall set off to head to town to find Prospero and ask him what is going on.

It is nightfall. The somber sky was still. No movement, no sound from the seaside, it was utterly pure silence that sent a chilling shiver up my spine and made the hairs on the back of my neck stand straight up. Annabel, ever since you have passed I have not stepped foot into town. What if the townspeople really do think I have gone mad, I chuckled, what if I have gone mad? I mean, it's so foolish of me to talk to someone who has passed, right? It is time. I slowly put one arm in and then the other arm in my jet black trench coat as I walked out of the house. Before I fully stepped foot out of the door I glanced back and took a look at the house and whispered, "I'll be back soon, my sweet angel."

My attempt was to go into town without being noticed and to quickly find Prospero. As I walked, there still was no sound. No wind, no sound of the waves coming in on the seaside, not even the slightest noise of a cricket chirp. It takes a good twenty minutes to walk to town. Time passes, and still no sound, but I finally reach town.

Not one light was on, every store door was wide open, not one person appeared to be anywhere; no sound, just complete silence from the farthest distance. As I began to walk further down the middle of town to see if anyone was there, I looked down and noticed at my feet a small piece paper. I bent over and picked it up, and there appeared a drawn picture of a person. My mouth dropped with fear, and I couldn't yell nor speak; my hand reached up and covered my mouth. The paper was titled in huge letters that read, "WANTED: Wanted for Prospero Raven escaped from the sanitarium and is wanted in question for five murders. Please take precaution and leave now."

Were my eyes playing tricks on me? I made my way to the park, gathering my thoughts, as I sat on the park bench it began to make sense, Prospero has not come to see me in three weeks. There is not a soul in town, and I have an awful feeling in my chest as if someone was stabbing me and twisting the knife in my flesh. Then there came a scuffling noise from behind me. I slowly glanced around my shoulder, and there stood Prospero laughing devilishly with a sinister look.

He leans in and whispers in my ear, "This can be your greatest story of all," as the piano wire stole my last breath. Prospero peered into my eyes and said, "Now I can finally give the world the Edgar Allen Poe they deserve."

My body was found in the exact spot on the park bench. I was dressed in Prospero's clothes which were too small for me. Now me and my sweet Annabel can rest in peace together.

Prospero Raven now lives in my house and pretends to be *the* Edgar Allen Poe. But to this day, no one knows how I died, so now you know about the Real Death of Edgar Allen Poe.

High School Short Story
FOUNDER'S CHOICE AWARD

Aaron Walton is a tenth grade student at Roane County High School.

Monster

People say that monsters aren't real.

I beg to differ.

Most of my life I've believed in the creatures of the shadows; the thing hiding in the closet, the quiet figure lurking beneath my bed waiting to snatch any feet dangling over the edge.

As a young child these beings haunted my imagination causing me to take refuge underneath the covers on countless nights. But, with time, my feelings towards them changed from fearing their presence to longing for their company.

You see, when I was eight, my mother passed away from breast cancer, and since my father left us when I was only a few months old, my grandmother took me in and raised me by herself. Her name was Mabel, but I called her Nana. She was a very frail woman, but she could put you back in your place if she needed to. We weren't very close before my mother's passing and our relationship didn't get any better after it. She didn't hate me but she wasn't much interested in me either.

When I moved in with her, the monsters followed and made themselves at home.

Since Nana lived in a different state, I was forced to change schools in the middle of the year. The other kids didn't take much of a liking to me. I don't blame them. I don't like myself either. They didn't avoid me because I looked funny or I was rude. They avoided me because it's as if my sorrow and misfortune built a wall keeping everyone out. I could sense it and I knew they could too.

So, I sat alone on the edge of the playground watching my peers smile and laugh as I envied their ability to be so utterly carefree. I doubt any of them have lost as greatly as I have. I lost my home, my friends, my mother, and my ability to grow up and live life like an ordinary child.

The only thing I didn't lose were the monsters. Which, I suppose, wasn't a bad thing.

They kept me company during the long hours of sitting in my room as I colored worn coloring books with broken crayons. I couldn't exactly see them, but I could sense their presence like when you think you're alone but you still feel a thousand eyes watching your every move.

Sometimes I would even talk to them, but of course they didn't respond. I was a very lonely child.

As I matured, I could tell that the monsters were slowly fading away, and by the time I was in junior high, I became accustomed to their absence. Soon enough, I started to doubt their existence and blamed what I had previously believed on my overactive imagination as a young and introverted child. Even the thought of such creatures seemed childish and stupid.

That was until I met Mr. Corfrigus.

At first, he came to me in a dream. He started out as a black smudge hiding in the hazy landscape of the dream world but slowly, within each dream I had, the dark, blurry figure became more detailed as he leisurely crept his way closer to where I stood. When he got near enough, the first thing I noticed was a black, wide brimmed hat that hid his eyes. He wore a full length ebony cloak that swayed back and forth. The thing walked hunched over with staggered movements as he made his way over. When I had first looked at his face from a distance, I thought he had dark skin, but when I got a closer view, his skin is actually a translucent, pale color and he appeared to be wearing a black leather mask over where its nose and mouth should be. He has what looks like metal vents coming out both sides of the mask, but why?

When he was finally arm's length away, he stopped. Corfrigus was the same height as me. However, his hat still covered his eyes. I could see vapor force its way out of the holes in his mask with each breath he took. Without the puffs of steam, you probably wouldn't be able to tell if he was breathing or not. He was so still.

After he stood in front of me for a couple of minutes, seeming to be studying me, he finally spoke, and when he did, I was surprised. "Hello, I suppose you must be wondering who I am and what I am doing here, but do not worry yourself. I do not wish to harm you. You may call me Mr. Corfrigus, and I request your help," he said with a voice so clear and smooth, like a proper Englishman, even with the mask on. It took me a second to realize that it had come from the thing in front of me. He wanted me to help him?

"Why?" I questioned.

"My dear child, I wish for your assistance because you're unlike the other children. You're special"

"What do you mean, I'm 'special'?"

"What I mean, is that *you* are the only one who can free me from this prison," he said, gesturing to the landscape in my dream.

"Why are you here?" I asked, very confused.

"You see, I'm a lost soul. When I passed away, my spirit strayed from 'the light' so I wandered aimlessly, and I ended up here, inside your head. Please, will you help free me?"

"What do you need me to do?"

"First, I need you to promise that regardless of anything, you will help me," he said with all seriousness as he held out his long, pale, bony hand for me to shake.

I hesitated for a moment. I decided to play along since it's just a dream. It's not like anything bad could happen. If anything seems off, I could just wake myself up and that would be the end of it. Also, his pure voice was very convincing. "I promise."

I took Mr. Corfrigus's hand and shook it. Immediately, a blinding light was emitted from where our palms touched. The light illuminated his face and I could see his eyes. They were a crimson red with the pupils slit like a snake's. I could tell that he was growing taller with each second while still hanging on to my hand with a vicelike grip. He had to be at least eight feet tall. Frightened, I tried to pull my hand back, but his grasp was too tight. Then I tried waking up, but it was no use.

"Too late to back out now," he said with a wild look in his eyes. His entrancing voice was replaced with a hellish cry. It sounded like nails being scratched on a chalkboard with every word he spoke.

Once the light dimmed away, he loosened his grip and shoved me to the ground. "You're mine now," he screeched with a satisfied tone.

"W-what do you mean?" I questioned hysterically.

"I own you now. Until you set me free from this penitentiary, you must do what I say or else I promise to make you wish for the bittersweet mercy of death. Got that?"

"W-what do you need me to do?"

"Take a life, spill some blood, kill somebody," he cackled.

I look down in disbelief. This thing wants me to kill someone? I can't kill anybody! I'm not a murderer!

I calmed myself down and remembered that it's only a dream. This isn't real and Mr. Corfrigus isn't real. It's just a bad dream. A horrible nightmare.

"Is it now?" he questioned with a slight smirk visible even with the mask on.

I didn't stop to ask him how he knew what I was thinking before I attempted to force myself awake again.

My eyes popped open wide awake as I sprang up from my bed with my heart pounding against my ribcage.

I took a deep breath and told myself that it was just in my head. I don't have to kill anybody, and I'm nobody's slave. It was just a sick and twisted dream.

"Are you so sure?"

I jerked back and slowly turned my head to where I heard the voice. To the right of me, standing at my bedside was the thing that demanded me to carry out such a horrendous task.

Its dark body loomed over mine.

I darted to the opposite side of the bed to try to get as far away as possible from the wretched creature. Although his hat shaded his entire face, his eyes burned through the shadows like fiery coals fueled with sadistic amusement. He glared at me with such ferocity that I froze in place.

"Thought you could get away from me didn't you?" he howled.

I managed to force out a few words. "H-how are y-you here?"

"You should be careful with the promises you make little one," he said with a devilish look.

"I've gone insane!" I screamed as I clutched my head and shut my eyes. I can't believe this is happening to me. I never thought that I'd be the one to have my mind unravel before me.

Only crazy people see and hear things that aren't real. I'm not crazy, am I?

After a few minutes, I opened my eyes and saw that Mr. Corfrigus was gone. There was a gentle knock on my door.

"Dear, are you all right? I heard you yell, and I became worried. Please, come out. Let me see you," said a soft spoken voice on the other side of the door. It sounded like it belonged to Nana, but I couldn't be too sure of myself. She's always called me by my first name, never "dear."

Adrenaline rushed through my veins. It could be Corfrigus.

Building up my courage, I grabbed my metal bat and headed over to the door. I slightly hesitated before turning the knob. There, I'm met with the demon I feared. The beast that haunted my mind. The thing that's making me question my own sanity.

He looked down at me, and I could tell he was grinning.

"Foolish child. How stupid can you be?" he said with an earth shattering voice.

At this point, my blood was boiling with hatred. I no longer feared this thing. I despised him.

"This is it! I've had enough! I'm either gonna end you or die trying!" I screamed with fury-filled determination.

"Oh really?" he said sarcastically.

I swung the bat with all of my strength. I put every ounce of my hate into that one blow and it landed against his midsection with a satisfying thump. To my great surprise, Corfrigus staggered backwards, devastated by the hit. I noticed that he was getting dangerously close to the edge of the staircase. I rammed him again in the stomach with the metal bat and that did the job.

Corfrigus tumbled down the staircase with his body contorting in all different directions and the sound of bones cracking. I look away and once everything quieted down, I look back and see a collapsed mass at the bottom.

"Can you be so sure?" said a voice directly behind me. I knew who it was. I could feel his hot breath hitting the back of my neck.

Oh no. Nana.

I didn't even look behind me before I rushed down the stairs to my grandmother. When I reached the bottom, I could see a pool of blood gathered beneath her lifeless body.

"Nana? Nana! Wake up! Oh God, please, wake up! No! No no no no no no no!"

Tears welled up in my eyes as I tried to shake her corpse. For some reason I thought that maybe she would wake up and everything would be okay, but she was gone. I noticed her blood on my hands, and I couldn't bear to look at it. It showed me what I have become. A murderer.

I rushed to the bathroom and rinsed the blood off. I became immersed in watching the water spiral down the drain and wished that I could escape with it. I looked up to the mirror to try to compose myself, and what I saw forced me out a shriek of terror.

In the mirror, my reflection had been replaced by the devil that tormented me for too long. We glared at each other with equal hatred.

"You set me free," said the creature in the mirror.

Then, to my horror, I realized something.

Instead of fighting the monster, I'd become the monster.

Middle School Short Story
FIRST PLACE

Lillian Bacon is an eighth grade student at Midway Middle School.

Bad Times

"If you walk outside, you will find a world that will destroy our entire civilization, the economy we fought to make perfect. That means we must shut down all energy sources. We can no longer support them. We also cannot offer you protection. Please find ways to fend for yourselves. We are ripping up the Constitution! It is inevitable that the world is a place that we never wanted to see or imagine. The times are changing, and we shall call it the Bad Times," the president announced in a monotone voice, knowing his country would never be the same.

His speech played again and again on the country's radios until the constant static turned into a low buzz of nothingness. The people of America had always imagined themselves being heroes when things became bad. However, most of them covered their windows and stayed inside like cowards. They didn't want to see their ruined homeland. They didn't want to see the evil that had made it ruined.

The evil was the apocalypse, and the ones who were too afraid to see that would not survive.

*

Ashton hurried down the sidewalk with non-perishable groceries in her arms. For some reason, her principal had announced that school was over early due to a sudden natural disaster. After exiting the building, she found cars speeding down the main roads and children riding bicycles to quickly make it home. What if her sister, Carly, hadn't made it home? What if her mother had been swallowed by a storm or her father was being encased in a crack in the earth? The girl shook her head as she made it to her neighborhood's entrance. There was no time to think about the what ifs in the current situation. She just needed to get home.

Ash slowed her pace as she came closer to her house. The teenager made herself not think about her mother who was locked in an office cubicle or her father in his jail cell, begging in vain to be released. She reached the front door and twisted the door knob, not thinking about the vacant area around her. She stepped over the door frame, closed the door behind her, and sighed in relief. She had made it home.

"Carly!" the blonde teenager yelled as she walked into the kitchen. Ash frowned in frustration after setting the preserves down. Carly usually answered with her head stretching out of her bedroom. "It's Ashton!" the girl called again. Again, there was not a response. Ash felt fear tingle down her spine, so she cautiously walked to Carly's room.

"Hello?" she said after entering the colorful room. She walked toward a small bed covered with stuffed animals of many sizes. Ashton dropped to the floor and looked into the darkness under the bed. Ash did not know that a disease, the natural disaster, had found its way into Carly's first grader teacher's system before she released her students. The teacher had taken an eager bite out of Carly's wrist, which had sent the children running out of the school with panic painted on their faces. Carly had made it home before collapsing in the closet of her bedroom ...

As Ash sat up, a quiet groan came from behind her. Her black eyes became big, and all the calm inside of her was released into the atmosphere. Ashton slowly stood up and turned around. A small figure stood unsteadily on the pink carpet a few feet away from the bedroom door. Ashton gasped and whispered, "Carly?"

Carly did not look like her normal self, a smaller and more gentle version of Ashton. She looked grotesque with dried blood covering her gray skin and school uniform. Her blue eyes were clouded and bloodshot, and there were teeth marks on her left wrist. Ashton tried to back away from the creature, but her limbs were frozen in fear. Carly began to advance toward her unmoving sister at the speed of a snail, groaning the whole time.

Ashton gave up and let her body sink to the floor. She was too paralyzed in fear to protect herself. She closed her eyes and waited for the worst.... Eventually the creature bent down and breathed heavily into Ashton's ear before poising its mouth in the perfect position to bite.

*

Ashton eventually came to, feeling numb and confused. She looked around at blurry surroundings and staggered into a standing position. She inhaled, and a surprising groan escaped her throat. Voices erupted into the girl's mind, saying, "So hungry. Must eat." The voice was not her own, but she didn't know that. She could not remember anything. Ashton put a hand on her stomach and clumsily walked out of a bright, unfamiliar room.

Outside of that room she found a hallway that led to a larger room with a couch and a blank TV screen. Ashton inhaled once again and found herself trying to turn a door knob. In defeat, she staggered into a nearby window with a large crash and fell onto the front lawn. Ignoring the glass that cut through her thin skin, she stood up and followed the scent of something living.

The girl hobbled along the cracked sidewalks of her neighborhood, identifying her species with a turn of the head. Her head eventually turned to an elderly man sitting on a nearby bench with a silver trumpet pressed against his lips. A loud sound escaped the instrument, forcing Ash to growl at the man. The trumpeter ignored her and continued playing the sad melody of 'Taps.'

Drool rolled down the injured creature as the man played on, heat escaping his body. Ash took an instinctive path toward the man and began to devour his flesh with loud groans in between swallows. The man did not complain. He simply played on until air could no longer escape him.

Hours later, Ashton backed away from the body with no emotion present inside of her. Her hunger was not eradicated, but her body was slightly stronger. 'Taps' played on in her mind as she staggered toward another meal and a group of her kind. She let herself walk out of the sunset-covered neighborhood, ready to fulfill a life of uncontrollable evil in the Bad Times.

Middle School Short Story
SECOND PLACE

Rebekah Brooks is an eighth grade student at Midway Middle School.

The Agent

Jacob's silent alarm woke him up, and he got out of bed counting the time that he had left to himself inside of his head. "Two clicks to get dressed," Jacob thought to nobody special but himself as he got dressed, putting on dark blue jeans, a black tee shirt, solid black socks, and his darkly colored shoes.

"Thirty tocks left," Jacob declared as he walked out of the door and mounted his dirty motor bike. Jacob declared inside of his own mind, "I have to hurry because I have a very important job to do," as he pulled up to the small, unstable cavern that held his hostage, emergency pack, and supplies on his small but efficient motor bike.

Jacob then put the small, whimpering boy inside of the sidecar and injected him with the liquid tracker, then grabbed the pack and supplies while the child was still crying softly but steadily in the background.

Jacob slowly mounted the small and unstable bike and said to the small and frightened boy, "Your name is B14. Now stop your crying and straighten up because you are my problem now, and I will not hesitate to throw you off this bike if you annoy me."

The boy, now known as B14 by Jacob, got quiet but decided to ask a few questions. "Who are you and where in the world are you taking me?" These where just a few of the questions he would ask that dark and stormy night.

Jacob allowed himself to sigh because now he was supposed to tell this mysterious boy the truth, that he was B1 and that they were brothers, both built in a lab. "My name is Jacob, but my experiment number is B1. I am your big brother, and I am here to protect you, then I have to take you to headquarters," Jacob said.

Not much more was said between the two boys until they reached the safe house, and only then did Jacob say to the boy his warning, which was to keep quiet and follow straight behind him.

"B1 reporting for duty," he said to one of the eight guards on duty at the six-foot-tall electric chain link and barbed wire gate.

"You may enter, young ones," was the only response the two boys had any hope of getting in return from the fit old man.

The small room the two boys then entered was dark and gloomy, so both B1 and B14 were equally thrilled to be going into the brightly lighted elevator across the hall. "Where are we going?" was the only question the small boy, once more frightened, dared to ask.

"First, I get to take you to the lab and get someone to chip you, then I will take you to the conference room and we tell you who you are."

"What are you talking about, who is we?" the boy, now curious, asked almost immediately.

"That is classified," B1 answered just as quickly when they stepped into the lab. Jacob sighed. Since everybody was busy, he would have to give the boy a needle. Jacob gestured for B14 to go to the worn and used up lab table in the middle of the large and unforgiving room, and naturally, of course, the boy did exactly as he was told. Inserting the large needle, B1 look a deep breath and pushed down the plunger, injecting the permanent liquid tracker into the small, nervous child.

"You two mean to tell me, a human child, that I am an incredibly hostile bionic robot droid that is designed to destroy the universe and everything in it? That now I have to live here until further notice?" the boy asked in disbelief.

"Yes," Jacob answered, "but later you can be hired as a double agent like me. You can also choose to work inside of the company."

"Ok," stated the child, "I will stay so I can be like you, brother."

"Good, because I have to leave now," said Jacob as he left his only brother behind. Jacob knew this was better for both of their benefits, but it did not make leaving his brother and never seeing him again any better.

Middle School Short Story
THIRD PLACE

Madi Thompson is a sixth grade student at Harriman Middle School.

Why I'm No Longer a Babysitter

It was my first day babysitting, Oh joy! My parents were walking out of the house as my sister held on to their feet, and I even think my dog cried a little. I mean, am I that bad at babysitting? My parents pulled out of the drive way. My sister turned and gave me the look. If you don't know what the look looks like, it looks like a mix between I'm going to cry very loudly where everyone is going to hear, and I'm going to make your day horrible! At least my dog was happy. I think?

We went inside, and my sister ran to her room like a cheetah. I wondered what she was planning. I was sitting on the couch when I heard the door open. I ran out the door only to see my sister running for the dog as the dog is chasing the mailman. I was only on the couch for a second.

I ran through the field chasing a dog and my sister! I mean, I look crazy! I wonder what my neighbors were thinking. I finally caught up to them, and then my sister fell. Picture this, we were running through a field full of cows and something brown is on her face. Oh no! The good part was

I saw my friend from school start chasing the dog too, and we finally got the dog and went inside.

I was so frustrated, but I ran a bath and told my sister to get in while I started washing her laundry. I went into the laundry room, started soaking her clothes, and then heard a big bang come from the kitchen. What now?

I ran into the kitchen and into a huge cloud of black smoke. My sister had put popcorn in the microwave for 15 minutes! I ran to the microwave, but it was too late, the microwave was on fire, and the kitchen was a wreck! I got a cup of water and put it out, but not before the fire department showed up at the same time my parents were pulling in the driveway.

My sister started running out the door towards them, most likely to tell them everything. I was right, she told them what happened, and they found the kitchen a mess, and their microwave destroyed. Instead of getting my babysitting money, my parents got a new microwave and fresh paint for the kitchen. That was the worst day ever, and the reason I'm no longer a babysitter!

Elementary Short Story
FIRST PLACE

Abigail Mynatt is a fifth grade student at Bowers Elementary School.

Escaping a Concentration Camp

I ran past the guards, away from the dogs, and towards the barbed wire fence. As I ran, the guards chased after me. I spotted the hole in the fence, got on my hands and knees and crawled towards the hole. As I was crawling my old, raggedy pajama shirt was caught on the fence . Then I knew I would be caught trying to escape a concentration camp.

I wish I could explain what was happening but this is how it went. My mother, my father, my best friend Katelyn, and I, Esmeralda, were all leaving because of the Nazi soldiers. My entire family was Jewish, and so was my friend. While we were leaving, all of us were taken to different concentration camps. Luckily my friend and I were together. Days went by, people were taken from their cabins and didn't come back. I knew I would be taken next. Weeks went by, but I was never taken.

"Get up, you useless Jews!" yelled an angry soldier.

I bolted awake from my deep sleep and ran from my cabin . Katelyn was already up and calling my name. "Esmeralda , come here!" she yelled, her eyes filled with fear.

"What do you need?" I asked. "We need to make a plan to break out of this horrid place!" It was at that moment that the quiet girl whom I loved like a sister became a girl who would do anything for freedom.

We talked as much as we could after and during work, after about a week we finally had a plan. We didn't know that many other Jews heard our plan. Our plan was I would help Katelyn out of the fence without getting caught, a day later I would go the same way out, and we would meet at our old house. The night finally came, Katelyn hugged me and said the most loving things, "I never knew my family, but now I know I have a sister." A tear ran down her cheek, and we darted toward the fence.

I had found a hole in the fence and dug to make it bigger. As soon as I did that I heard boots marching along. I helped Katlyn under the fence and she ran away. The soldiers walked right by me and didn't notice me slip back in my cabin.

The next night it was my turn to break out, but the next night when I was crawling under the fence my old, ripped shirt was caught on the fence. "Help, help!" I screamed at the top of my lungs. Then I saw a tall shadow. The shadow bent down next to me and unhooked my shirt and stuck out her hand to pull me up. As soon as she did that I made out her face, it was Katelyn! I smiled, but the guards grabbed lights and were searching the woods.

We crawled on our stomachs as fast as we could. Finally we found my old home, but in the distance we heard gunshots and screams. We ran out to see the Nazis had shot the Jews who heard about Katlyn's plan but refused to tell where we went. They gave their lives so we could live. We ran far away from that camp and were never found by the soldiers. We later freed many more people from the camps. We went to my parents' camp but never found them. I took it upon myself that they were killed by the evil Nazi soldiers who tried to stop our escape.

Katelyn said, "God will take care of them and us, always."

I never learned what happened to my parents, but Katelyn and I were family enough. We made many more escape plans for others to escape concentration camps.

Elementary Short Story
SECOND PLACE

Layla Vowell is a fourth grade student at Dyllis Springs Elementary School.

Joe Joe and the Bees

Once there was a monkey named Joe Joe. One day, he was having fun with his friends and felt a sting. He noticed it was a bee, so he climbed up in his tree and hid.

After a few hours, he said to himself, "No more hiding! I am going to kill that pesky little bee!" He took a jar and tried to catch it, but that didn't work.

Next, he rolled up some paper and tried to squish it, but that also didn't work. Finally he asked his friends to help, and soon after that all the monkeys he knew were helping!

A few minutes after, the bee mysteriously just ... disappeared! All the monkeys looked and looked and looked ... but still never found it. All the monkeys were relieved that the bee was gone, and they got a good night's sleep.

But when they woke up... an entire swarm of bees was coming for them!

All the monkeys were staring in fright at all the bees. All of them thought, "If we can barely get rid of one bee, then how are we going to get rid of an entire swarm of them!" They could barely move they were so scared!

Except one: Joe Joe. He was scared, too, but thought he could get rid of the bees. So he took a rolled up stack of paper and started to squish some of the bees one at a time. Once the other monkeys saw him doing that, they started to join in too ... just like last time. That didn't seem to be working. All the monkeys were still very scared... but they kept on trying.

The monkeys decided they were going to have to move to a new home. They all thought it was so sad. The leader of all the monkeys told them to gather up all of their stuff and head west. Thankfully the bees didn't follow.

After a couple of days, one monkey started to get sick, and they were all tired. They had traveled hundreds or even thousands of miles. They didn't even sleep the last couple of nights. They stopped to get water once or twice, but that didn't really help.

Joe Joe said they needed to rest. And the leader said they could stop and rest here for the night. There were only two trees in sight, but they were big. One of them was smaller than the other, but that was good. The monkeys divided into two groups.

The first group was bigger so they went into the big tree. The second group was smaller, so they went into the smaller one.

In the morning, they gathered their stuff back up and kept moving. After exactly three hours, Joe Joe spotted another jungle. Their lives were saved!

All the sick monkeys could be treated, and the others could get some more rest. They finally found a new place to call home! So they all settled in. The families all got to find a tree they liked and stay there.

They let Joe Joe's family have the biggest and best tree because he was the one that found and caused them to have a new home. They all loved their new jungle, and there weren't any bees in sight.

Elementary Short Story
THIRD PLACE

Allbree Hanshaw is a fourth grade student at Bowers Elementary School.

The Dummy

Once upon a time there was a little boy. His name was Jake. He loved ventriloquist acts ever since he was five. Jake wanted a dummy so when he grows up he can be a ventriloquist person.

He thought ventriloquist acts were so funny. Jake was so excited because tomorrow was Christmas. He went to sleep and had a bad dream that he had a ventriloquist dummy and it kept making fun of him and it grabbed him and said a special spell.

The spell was called reverse the curse. Slappy said, "It's time you feel how it is to be a dummy."

Jack started turning into a dummy at 9:00pm and at 12:00pm, he was a full dummy. Jake woke up and screamed. He said, "Yes, it was just a dream," so Jake went back to sleep.

Jake woke up the next morning but couldn't move his legs or body. Jake screamed and said, "I'm a dummy."

He called his friend Jerrik. Jerrik said hello, but it was too late. Jake was already a full dummy, and the dummy was a human, but no ordinary human – he was Jake. The dummy Jake wondered how he was a dummy, but then it hit him. He tried to scream, but he couldn't.

Slappy came up to him and said, "Let's see how it feels to be thrown and broken. Slappy threw Jake. Jake flew across the room and landed outside the window, but then Slappy ran downstairs and picked up the dummy and saw a piece of paper sticking out of his pocket and Slappy grabbed it.

Slappy went back upstairs and put on his pajamas and went to sleep. Slappy set the dummy on the desk next to the paper then Slappy went to sleep. The dummy tried and tried to reach the paper, but then he saw a sparkle and the sparkle turned him back to a human.

Jake grabbed the paper and said the curse, but it didn't work. Jake said the spell backwards and a big cloud of smoke came out of nowhere, and everything went back to normal.

Jake woke up and said, "I'm a human again," but the dummy was still a human.

Slappy ran outside and said, "You will never catch me."

Jake ran as fast as he could and caught Slappy. Jake said a spell, "From now till then and then till now from this point forwards I turn this day backwards," and Slappy turned back into a dummy. Jake said, "It's all over now."

Jake threw Slappy away, and now he could live in peace. Jerrik came over and said, "What happened? Why didn't you call back?"

Jake said, "Ummm, I was busy," and they both laughed, and everything was better after that.

Elementary School Short Story
A. NONNIE MUSS AWARD

Luke Gunter is a fifth grade student at Midtown Elementary School.

The Gate

Chapter 1

"Tyron wake up!" exclaimed Tyron's mother.

Tyron replied, hardly awake, "Wha…?"

"It's school today!" Tyron's mother stated.

Tyron said, "Crap!" He jumped out of bed, got his clothes on, and zoomed out the door, slamming the door behind him.

He was in the gym line while a teacher was calling grades. "Good; I got here in the right amount of time!" Tyron said to himself.

Chapter 2

His homeroom teacher, Mr. Blitz, had taken them outside for free time when Tyron saw a golden gate behind the playground, but no one else seemed to notice it. He gathered some of his friends: Fred, a very smart kid; Ryan, the strongest in the grade; Taylor, the kind of girl who likes to be the leader; and lastly Bob, another strong kid.

Tyron took them to the gate and demanded, "Look at this!"

"What the crap is this?!" yelled Bob.

"A gate, you son of the biscuit!!" screamed Taylor.

"But where?" asked Fred.

Tyron replied, "There's only one way to find out where it leads, we go in."

"W-Wait up!" stated Bob. So the rest of them went with Tyron. There was a huge *slam* behind them; the gate closed and disappeared!

"Tyron, you big, foolish idiot!!!!!!!!" yelled Ryan.

"Shut the crap up!" demanded Tyron.

"Hmmmmmm, I've got some new puppets to play with," muttered a strange voice.

Chapter 3: Destiny?

"Where are we?" asked Fred.

"I don't know for sure, but it looks like h-hell!" responded Tyron, struggling.

"Tyron, look – a chest," said Fred.

"I will open it," said Bob. He grabbed the top and the bottom and yanked it open!! There was a shotgun, a battle axe, a staff, a katana, and a pair of daggers.

"I call the shotgun!" stated Ryan.

"Then I'll get the battle axe!" said Bob.

"I will have the staff!" exclaimed Taylor.

"Let me get the daggers," stated Fred.

Tyron yelled, "Yes, I get the katana!!"

"Servants, go easy on them, I want to see how they do!" said a strange voice.

"Yes, my lord!" said the minions.

Chapter 4: The battle!!

"Wait – look! Two figures are coming and it looks like they are flying!" exclaimed Ryan.

"Why, hello kids!" said the first monster.

"I guess this will be the time to test our weapons out?" asked Taylor.

Tyron answered, "I guess so!"

So they fought.

"AAKKKKKKKKKKKKKKKKKKKKK"!! exclaimed Bob.

"Aidan, NOOOOOO!" yelled Taylor. "Stay with me – don't die already!"

"I'm sorry, I just can't stay awake!" whispered Bob. Then Bob slowly died in Taylor's arms!

"No – we just started this and we already lost someone!" cried Tyron.

The first creature chuckled, *"Well, that is so sad – NOT!"*

"Shut the crap up, you big creeps!" exclaimed Ryan.

The monsters glared at us. Then Tyron smirked and said, "There's still more of us." Then Tyron went rampage on them.

"Only one thing to do – open the gates!" said the second monster.

"Why would you do that?" asked Tyron.

The monsters just ignored him and then let the gates open.

"I have a bad feeling," said Ryan.

"Oh, nice plan, servants!" said the voice. While the gates opened, the monsters called a whole army of creatures.

Chapter 5: Reveal

The numerous amount of monsters all went.

"Oh, sugar honey iced tea!" shouted Tyron.

"Really - you have to say that at this time?" glared Ryan.

Monsters were everywhere, torturing or killing people that they see. The voice muttered. *"Well, I guess it's time to reveal myself."* The king of monsters flew to Tyron.

Chapter 6: The end

"Hell is coming to invade. Oh how rude of me – my name is Blitz. But you could call me your all eternal lord!!" said Blitz. After seven hours of death, Tyron was the only man on Earth, and he knew it! He was in the shelter, then he heard a knock!!!!!!

High School Poetry
FIRST PLACE

Abby Jackson is a twelfth grade student at Roane County School.

Education

The system is flawed and the kids are suffering.

Our heads are filled with facts, yet we're learning nothing.

Anxiety is through the roof, confidence is plummeting.

Life has been short, yet it feels like it's ending.

I'm seventeen, but I'm treated like a child.

I'm smart, but I'm being talked down to.

I'm stressed beyond belief, but I'm lacking motivation.

I'm graduating, but I still feel like I'm drowning.

Education no longer has the same definition.

Education has changed for the worst, not the better.

Education is all about memorization, not real information.

Education is no longer about learning, it's about cramming.

I will not let my education define me.

The change in the system begins with me.

Public education has deeply affected me.

But I know that the change will happen, and it will be with me.

High School Poetry
SECOND PLACE

Kylie Richardson is a tenth grade student at Oliver Springs High School.

Imperfect Scars

Fragile like glass

One mistake and she'll crack.

    Inconceivably whole.

    Invisibly imperfect.

Blue eyes fringed with hatred, like lies on cracked lips.

Opened to a world of loneliness and pain.

Veiled scars basked in hooded cover

    infect and possess her soul.

Inconspicuous pain, like a wave crashing through the soul,

    rises to crimson drops of serenity.

Slowly refine to rivers of white veins.

Feelings lick along caramel dappled skin and reside

    with wind swept breaths

        as a solitary tear rolls down her face.

Concealed scars are the hardest to heal.

Her mind is violent. Her screams are silent.

A lonely girl with a vacant stare.

Scars on her body, scars on her soul.

    Eternally broken.

High School Poetry
THIRD PLACE

Mari Claire Crass is a tenth grade student at Oliver Springs School.

Big Brother

The day started out just like no other,

A story about three sisters, one brother.

We left you that day feeling all right,

Not knowing what would happen later that night.

We all tried to call hoping you weren't there too,

But little did we know what had happened to you.

My big brother who once was so strong and so bold,

Was suffering, was dying, at just 20 years old.

When we got to the hospital, I started to cry.

I remembered the moments I so carelessly let by.

All the times you were there to keep me on track.

All those memories I may never get back.

Then came the news about two of our friends.

So happy, so young, but their time had come to an end.

I started to panic; I started to doubt,

But God had a plan that none of us knew about.

As they took us back to finally see you,

I wasn't prepared to see what you had been through.

For the person I saw wasn't my brother.

He wasn't laughing or joking like we did with each other.

You laid there helpless, not breathing on your own.

I wanted the brother I had left back at home.

When we stood there and spoke what could be goodbye,

We thought you couldn't hear us, but you started to cry.

My big brother was there under the scratches and bruises.

He had heard us talking, but only we knew this.

For this was God saying he would be alright;

That my brother wasn't leaving, no, not tonight.

Day by day you started to heal.

But I still couldn't believe that all this was real.

Our lives were changed that day in May,

And I still praise God that you got to stay.

For you never know when your time will come,

Or when life will make you worry some.

So treasure the people you care and love,

And always give thanks to our Lord above.

High School Poetry
FOURTH PLACE

Mathew Webb is a ninth grade student at Oliver Springs School.

The Right Track

I will always try my best to make good grades

Keep my dreams in sight and not let them fade

Be respectful, squash rumors, and not talk smack

It's hard to be a teenager and stay on the right track.

I won't drink and I won't do drugs

I won't be a loser or hang out with thugs

If you're young and stupid, some things you can't take back

I want to always make sure I stay on the right track.

It is easy to submit to pressure from a peer

Some may try to get you to smoke weed or drink beer

With others I sometimes question, "How do I stack?"

I try not to worry and keep on the right track.

Good character helps build a strong foundation

Who knows one day I may be a leader in this great nation

Making good decisions and trying not to slack

Is how I plan to stay on the right track.

Military academy is one of my big goals

As a citizen I will do my part and play my role

Achieving success in life and learning, "What is my knack?"

I will get there, as long as I stay on the right track.

Middle School Poetry
FIRST PLACE

Sydney Bryant is an eighth grade student at Midway Middle School.

Kids of Divorce

Here we go again, the screams and the shouts

Guessing that's how life works out

I like to pretend as if nothing is wrong

So I play along

Inside we feel so insecure

Don't feel bad, there's nothing time can't cure

What happened to richer or for poorer, for better or for worse

I look back at those photographs

You two, filled with joy and laughs

Perhaps I could have prevented this disaster

That disaster always seem to be faster

Seeing mom in tears

Scanning so many fears

Every night my eyes flood because I begin to cry

Here and there I hear a lie

I sat there, looking for a sign

Am I the one to blame for the 5th time

I'll treasure those memories, I wish you the best

I can only imagine the rest

Leaving the past in the past

But will they ever last

The last walk down memory lane finds us crying and alone

With nothing left but memories of our family and our home.

Middle School Poetry
SECOND PLACE

Emily Scott is an eighth grade student at Midway Middle School.

Little Demon

I have a little demon,

that lives inside my brain,

and when she gets excited,

they think that I'm insane.

She makes me mean and hateful,

in many, many ways.

It's then I tend to break things,

in my creepy little craze.

I try so hard to stop her,

but she groans, and groans, and groans.

She hides herself in my disguise,

so that no one ever knows.

Some think I've lost my mind,

and think it's such a shame.

My demon laughs protected,

while I take all the blame.

Why don't they ever notice,

that I'm not even me?

I guess my demon hides so well,

that people will never see.

Middle School Poetry
THIRD PLACE

Anna Fink is a sixth grade student at Midway Middle School.

Tonight

Tonight is the night

The night of my life

Decisions, decisions, left and right

The moon is like a candle in the night sky

Tonight is the night that I will decide

What path I will take

On my journey of life

I am scared yet so happy

At the same time

I am nervous that my decision

Will not be right

I cannot go back and change my choice

I must pretend I have no voice

I do not know where to start

But I hope that I can follow my heart

Will I go left or will I go right

On this terrific, terrifying night?

Elementary School Poetry
FIRST PLACE

Loretta Ketterer is a fifth grade student at Bowers Elementary School.

My Map of Peace

The way the grass sways

And the water flows

The way the sun lights up orange

And the stars glow pink

How purple paves our roads of love

And paths make a map

Together they make something

Something beautiful

They make something amazing

And something to cherish

That in my eyes will always be there

And that's my map of peace.

Elementary School Poetry
SECOND PLACE

Caiydend Grigsby is a fifth grade student at Bowers Elementary School.

One Spring Day

One sunny spring day I went out to explore

I thought to myself that I had to know more

So I ran through the woods to see what was there

I had to go fast, there was no time to spare

So I ran very swiftly like a jet through the sky

There were so many sights that money can't buy

I came upon a large field covered with flowers

I thought I could stay there for hours and hours

So I frolicked around like a happy baby deer

I wish all my friends could see this or be here

Then the day ended so no more laugh and play

But I'll always remember this sunny spring day.

Elementary School Poetry
THIRD PLACE

Evan Chen is a fifth grade student at Bowers Elementary School.

Spring is Here

Spring is here,

tree leaves grow,

spring is here,

melting snow.

Everything grateful,

nothing hateful.

Flowers blooming,

nothing glooming.

Winter is gone,

no cold fawn,

time for fun,

with the warming sun.

High School Essay
FIRST PLACE

Adrianna Hicks is a ninth grade student at Oliver Springs High School.

Dress Code

It is time, at last, to address an issue of personal expression that affects schools nationwide. Every day women are forced to change their outfits or go home because of how much skin they show, the reason being, "boys will be boys." Even though you may tell us this is the reason, shouldn't you teach your children not to objectify women? Why does society feel the need to make a woman cover up her knees or hide her collar bones in fear that we may be a distraction? Now, I speak for women that have been objectified but not by the boys, but by the people who deem it appropriate to tell us that they are trying to prevent others from thinking that way.

Well, let me be the first to inform you that we are absolutely more than a distraction. We are more than your sexualized form of teenagers. We are told that we must dress modest, but you believe that we would dress immodest if it was not in place? Instead of shaming women for their bodies, learn that women are not sexual objects. We should, in fact, stop teaching women to change because of fear of men, and teaching men to respect women. This is simply perpetrating rape culture.

I must address to you how strong my feelings are for this, as the days grow hotter, shorts and sleeves grow smaller. We are not immodest for showing skin above the knees, showing our shoulders or the straps of our bras. We should not be shamed for what we have been given. By sending a woman home or forcing her out of class to change, you are telling her that her clothes are more important than her education. But, if a boy shows his knees it's fine? It's okay if a boy breaks dress code but not a woman. Your dress code is sexist; I would rather be the "obnoxious feminist girl" than be complicit to my own dehumanization. I am a fourteen-year-old girl, if you are sexualizing me you are the problem.

Men are never told that their legs, arms, or stomachs are a problem for other people. They are seen as fellow humans and are rarely seen as something there for your sexual exploits. Telling a woman that it is her responsibility to allow boys to concentrate on their school work rather than on girls is making girls feel guilty for having a body. Confidence should be rewarded, not shunned. Please let us stop this body shaming toward women. I may be wrong on this, but I believe we must fight and voice our opinions for our rights.

If you don't like what I am wearing, don't look. My body is mine and making choices regarding it is my right. If you are distracted, control yourself and focus on all the things you may be doing instead of telling a teenage girl to hide her body so that she may not distract boys.

My shoulders are not being exposed for you.

High School Essay
SECOND PLACE

Emma Jackson is a tenth grade student at Oliver Springs High School.

Freedom to be Me

"We hold these truths to be self-evident: that all men are created equal; that they are endowed by their Creator with certain unalienable rights; that among these are life, liberty, and the pursuit of happiness." Written by Thomas Jefferson, a phrase used in the United States Declaration of Independence which was established on July 4, 1776. Today in America we still have patriots fighting for our freedoms such as freedom to worship, freedom to vote, and freedom to give your own opinion.

For example, freedom to worship gives me the right to choose my religion, what church to attend, and the privilege to choose a version of the Bible. It gives me the right to express my religious beliefs and opinions. Freedom of religion also lets me have the right to worship God or not, as I see fit. It also gives me the right to choose my denomination. Freedom of religion is important because it gives people the right to worship the way they want to.

Also, I know that one day when I am older I will be very thankful to vote. The reason why is because women did not always have the right to vote, they never had a chance to voice their own opinions. Today women have the right to promote a position of legal and social equality as well as men. I will also be able to vote for a party of my choice, Republican or Democratic. Years ago there just used to be male candidates. Now, there are women candidates who run for office as well.

As well as having the right to vote, I will also be thankful to give my own opinion. I will be able to voice my opinion on political issues, religious issues, and moral issues. To me, giving an opinion is important because having your own opinion makes you who you are. You will find many people that won't voice their opinion and are just influenced by what others have to say. Everyone has their own opinion, some people just choose not to express them. So basically having your own opinion is important because it makes you, you.

To sum up, freedom to worship, freedom to vote, and freedom to have your own opinions are the reasons why I am thankful to be an American. These freedoms are the reason why America is the "Land of the free and home of the brave." If it wasn't for our brave men and women risking their lives every day, we would not have a free nation like we do today. I value these freedoms because many lives were lost so that I and fellow Americans could be given the rights we have today.

Middle School Essay
FIRST PLACE

Blake Parks is an eighth grade student at Midway Middle School.

Learning Foreign Languages

It is obvious that in order to learn a foreign language, one needs to learn many, many words. But how many? Educated English native speakers have a vocabulary of about 20,000 to 50,000 word families, foreign learners need far fewer. The speaking vocabulary is usually said to be half of reading and writing vocabulary. Foreign learners of English only need about 3,000 to 5,000 word families to be quite competent in speaking and listening to English. This is great news for learners of English because their tasks are much easier than that of native speakers.

One of the reasons for this seemingly small number is the nature of words and the frequency with which they appear in a language. Not all words are equal because some words such as a, the, come, and so on are very common, whereas others such as parasol, bombastic, and edifice are relatively rare and are not met every day. It therefore seems clear that these frequent words should be among the first words to learn because they will be met most often and will be needed frequently in speech or writing. Thus the payoff for learning them is higher than for an average rare word. These words are often called General Service Vocabulary because these words are found in many kinds of situations and domains. This is a vocabulary of about 2,000 word families. These General Service words are found a very wide range of contexts such as in the medical world, novels, in scientific reports, in web pages, in daily conversation, and so on. Because these words appear in so many contexts they are extremely useful to almost all learners. It has to be remembered, of course, that each of these topic areas just mentioned has its own specialists or technological vocabulary, for example the words embolism and gastroenteritis and so on appear in medicine, hydrogen, and thermodynamics appear in science and engineering, and interferometer appears in astronomy.

Have you ever heard someone say that they can speak English and that is enough, because after all most people speak English? Well, to tell you the truth they would be wrong. There are a number of reasons why you should learn a foreign language. In our world today, only one fifth of the population speaks English. So, learning another language is important for both work and travel. It is also important for making real connections with people, and lastly it can give you a greater understanding of your own language. If you are traveling or work in a foreign country such as China, then you could survive with only speaking English. However, think how much easier everything would be if you could speak the local language. It would simply be easier to do anything and everything. It would be easier to find different places, ask for directions, and even order food. If you work in China, it will benefit you immensely if you can speak Chinese because then you would be able to work with all different types of employees, not just the ones that speak English, and this will give long-term career success.

More and more job advertisements are now specifying that they want second, third, and even fourth languages in some cases, and knowing more than one language opens up your prospects in a highly important way. Furthermore, as more and more companies begin to trade internationally, people are frequently beginning jobs for which they need no language skills, but then being asked to relocate abroad or offered a promotion that requires language skills. Therefore, it helps with career enhancement. Some people refute this claim by saying that there are plenty of other jobs available, but this is simply not the case anymore with the global recession and more countries being international.

The second reason that it is important to know more than one language is that it increases cultural awareness and allows you to communicate with different people. All good methods of learning languages also entail learning about another culture, especially when your language skills get to a higher level. This awareness allows people from different nationalities and religions to get along with each other better, which is very important given the high levels of immigration. Many countries with high immigration levels have trouble with a lack of integration, and this is often because of the language barrier, so people end up being segregated, staying in communities where their own language is spoken. Even those that say they don't care about meeting people of other cultures will have noticed these problems and should accept the importance of learning other languages.

In conclusion, regardless of the reasons why you would like to learn a new language, you should always allow yourself to explore new linguistic territories. Learning multiple languages will always serve to enhance your quality of life, and even if you never use that language in practical circumstances, you almost certainly will enjoy the time spent educating yourself. Language learning is unique in that you rarely have to spend much money to find a passionate instructor or fellow learner, and the adventure of understanding a new tongue is one experience you will not soon forget.

Middle School Essay
SECOND PLACE

Savanna Longmire is a seventh grade student at Midway Middle School.

Cellphone Usage at School

There are different views regarding the rights of a student to possess a cellphone while at school. I believe a student should be able to have his or her cellphone while at school if it is not a disruption during normal school hours. The student should be aware of the consequences if their cellphone becomes a distraction during class time. Students should practice responsible behavior regarding the privilege of having a cellphone at school. Students should have access to school policy regarding personal cellphone usage during school hours. It is the responsibility of both students and parents to adhere to this policy.

Advantages:

In my opinion, cellphones should be allowed for students to possess while at school. One of the reasons I feel this way is because a child should be able to stay in contact with their parents in case of an emergency. For example, if a natural disaster occurs, a child should know how to respond. A cellphone would provide a child the ability to communicate with a parent regarding alternate transportation methods if necessary.

Another reason they should be allowed is in case of a family emergency. In the event a parent or other family member was in an accident or another emergency situation, the parent would be able to inform the child and instruct them how to properly handle the situation. Cellphones would be an asset in a situation like this.

Cellphones should also be allowed for student safety. For example, in the event of a school shooting, students may use their cellphones to contact the proper authorities. There have been many incidents where a student using a cellphone could aid in the event of a crisis. Students could give police information about what they may have witnessed during an event, such as the location of the shooting, the description of the assailants, and information about the victims.

Cellphones also would be beneficial for students to have during class time as a learning tool. Students can use their personal smartphones to access the Internet, and use as calculators, stopwatches, timers, educational apps, and more.

Cellphones can also be used if a student is sick and has to be absent from school. Facetime and Skype can be used for students to listen and watch a lesson from their home if they cannot be at school. A student could also use his or her phone to contact a student in another classroom if necessary. Cellphones are important to access contact phone numbers and information that the school office may not have access to. These are reasons to support why cellphones should be allowed for students to use during school hours.

Disadvantages:

There are also reasons why cellphones would be a disadvantage for students to possess during school. Cellphones could be a major distraction. The simple alert tones for incoming calls, text messages, and social media notifications can be very distracting for both students and teachers. School policy would typically state that the cellphone must be in the off mode and placed in a locker, backpack, purse, or other similar personal carrying device; however, students are sure to forget this rule sometimes which may cause disruptions to class lesson time.

Cellphones can also be a way for students to cheat on exams. With the use of cameras on cellphones, students can photograph exams or answers to exam questions. Students may also photograph other students when the permission to do so is not given. Cameras on cellphones can cause a serious threat to personal rights. The Internet is also an outlet for students to access answers to tests. Most cellphones today have Internet access, which allows another way for students to cheat on tests.

Students who have cellphones during class may not be fully attentive to the lesson being presented. Constant texting and social media distractions is an impairment to learning. Students who are focused on the functions of their cellphones are not going to be as focused on their studies. There is also no way to deter students who use cellphones during class time from accessing inappropriate material on the Internet.

Cyber bullying is also another issue that should be addressed and understood when discussing the use of cellphones during school hours. Therefore, cellphones could be considered a huge hindrance to the learning process.

In conclusion, there must be proper communication between school officials, students, and parents when addressing the issue of cellphone use during school hours. Students and parents should be aware of the written school policy regarding this issue. Both should also be aware of the consequences for violating the cellphone usage policy. Students and parents may have a definite need to be in contact with one another throughout the school day. Certain circumstances and situations should be dealt with on an individual basis. If all parties involved can be responsible when dealing with cellphone usage, then cellphones can be an advantage for a student to possess during school. Carrying a cellphone to school and acting responsibly while doing so can indicate the maturity level of a student. Learning to abide by school policy and rules can greatly benefit a student's personal growth. Cellphones should be seen as a learning tool and aid instead of a distraction. Teachers and students should embrace the possibilities that cellphones can provide. Carrying a cellphone to school should always be considered a privilege and not a right.

Middle School Essay
THIRD PLACE

Amy Sellers is an eighth grade student at Midway Middle School.

Equal Rights

People have been fighting for equal rights for centuries. There have always been those who feel that they are superior to others. But we've come a long way since then. Unfortunately, women and men still have this problem. In today's society, men are still superior to women. The major question here is why? No one really knows why men are "better" than women or why men can't show emotions. But, in all reality, are these things really that fair or right?

Some say that the reason women are treated this way is because men are stronger. They can lift more and hold back their emotions better than women can. Since when has crying or getting mad made a person weak? Just because a woman doesn't lift weights or she doesn't do construction work, she isn't as strong? Women are strong, just not always in the same ways as men. A woman goes through cramps for a week and you would never know it. Cramps hurt, but they don't cry because they are strong enough to get through their day.

Women are physically strong too. Take Ronda Rousey as an example. She is a UFC fighter. She is stronger than a lot of men. If women are so strong, then why is hitting like a girl an insult? Children hear this said on a daily basis. People telling them that they hit like a girl, they run like a girl, they play like a girl. This hurts girls', some of them don't understand why it's an insult. That's because it shouldn't be. Women have been in and won the Olympics. The phrase "like a girl" should mean that you are powerful, strong, determined, diligent, smart, and beautiful.

Think about that word: Beautiful. Often times, women are considered pretty. But women are so much more than just one word or look. Why can't they be more than one thing? It's not a crime, but today they have to look great. A woman could tell you how to achieve time travel, but the first thing you would notice is her clothes, shoes, or purse, never her brains. It is so stereotypical to only see women as material. Men are noticed for the work they do. Even when women do the same work, they aren't treated the same.

They also aren't paid the same as men; women are payed less in most cases. This is insane because men and women all have bills to pay and things to get done. Our society seems to believe that men are stronger than women and that women are overflowing with emotion and don't deserve to be treated equally. Despite these things, men don't have it all that great either.

Men can't show what they feel. It's almost like they have to be emotionless and strong all the time. But in all actuality, they have feelings too. If someone says something rude to them, all they can do is fight. They can't get upset over it. If a woman cries, it's just another day. A man cries, and he is made fun of. People cannot seem to wrap their heads around the fact that they are made with feelings. Men are supposed to be able to cry and get mad without fighting.

Society has this image for everyone, that no one can have flaws and that we need to be picture-perfect all the time. But the thing about picture-perfect is that pictures are one second of time; not for seconds, minutes, hours, days, or weeks. One second. People can't be perfect all the time. That implies that they are one thing.

No man, nor any woman, could ever be perfect or just one thing. Men need to be accepted for having feelings, and women should be appreciated for their brains and brawn as well as their looks. People are taking looks too far. If on a daily basis, the people of America told someone how smart they are or how strong they are, the whole of society would be impacted on such a level that people could just be themselves. People could just let themselves shine, and they could be happy. If the people of this country and all over this world would stop judging people for what they see, and more on what is actually happening, there would be less suicides, less drug addicts, less of all these horrible things. Sadly, this will probably never happen because for society to accept you, you can't be real. You have to be fake.

But what if no one cared what society thought? What if everyone just went about their day? What if everyone was accepted? Saying this is impossible would be too easy, too simple. This nation is strong enough when we work together that we can do anything. This nation is full of strong women and men who care about what happens in the future.

It's all too easy to say that women cry all the time and they can't be anything but pretty. Men? They deserve to let their tears be seen. It makes them no less of a man. Not everyone can be themselves, which is really depressing if you think about it. Men don't always want to be strong, they sometimes want to be vulnerable. When will they be able to? Who is going to fix this wicked way of thinking?

Emma Watson told the United Nations council, "Ask yourselves, if not me, who? If not now, when?" Keep these thoughts in mind when you inadvertently look down on a woman for liking books more than magazines or judge a man for crying. Think of what is happening on the inside of these people. Men and women are equal. Period. No questions asked. Women and men have the same rights. If this is true, then why do we accept the ideals that society brings forth for us to follow? Why do we follow them?

Best of the Rest

Contests being what they are, not everyone who enters can get a prize. The judges of this competition always struggle to choose the "winners" when so many entries demonstrate so much talent and imagination.

Therefore, the following pages present what the Editors deemed to be the "Best of the Rest" of the entries received.

High School Short Story

Reagan Conley is a twelfth grade student at Rockwood High School.

Hacked

My body hit the ground hard, knocking the air from my lungs. I heard another loud thud beside me. Concord. His figure sprang up as quickly as it collapsed and whipped back toward the broken ice.

"Nick!" His voice was strangled with the truth his mind had yet to accept. Then came the sound of a foot landing in water. Damn. I pushed myself up, all four limbs flailing to get a grasp of the slick ground.

"Concord!" I yelled. He was already ankle deep in the below zero water. Forcing myself to ignore the sting on my own legs, I pressed my palm to his chest.

"No, we've got to save him! Let go of me!" Tears adorned his face, and I felt my own eyes begin to burn for him.

Using the last of my strength, I grabbed his hood and threw him backwards, falling down semi-on his chest. "Concord, he's gone."

"I know," he whispered before burrowing his head in my shoulder. I cried silently along with my best friend as sobs wracked his body. We stayed like that until nightfall.

In silence we got up and gathered the three backpacks. Briefly I remember seeing Nick throwing his pack to Concord as the ice cracked, saying it would explain everything. I pushed it aside. We started a fire a few yards from the bank. For a while we just sat and stared at Nick's backpack. I tried to focus on the faded North Face label, a brand from the Old World, instead of its owner, who I had watched train a rifle on his own nephew before slamming it into the ice. Concord was the one to reach for it. Inside we found an envelope. His hands were shaking too badly to open it, so he handed it to me.

"Concord, Noemie, if you're reading this, something went wrong during our escape to the rebel hideout. You're not going to understand this at first. Neither of you passed your Exam, and the government wants you dead for it. I was the one given the Order to eliminate you, so we got a head start. The test didn't evaluate your intelligence, that was its purpose in the Old World. It's used to ensure that each person was effectively Implanted on their sixteenth birthday. The Vaccine you got wasn't a shot. It was a surgical procedure that implanted a microchip into your brain in order to control your thoughts, memories, and decisions. Orders could then be sent to the Chip, which forced the Implantee to perform the task. The only problem was its ineffectiveness on certain individuals. They call us Hackers and consider us dangerous. That's why we are to be eliminated. They killed your father, Concord, he was one of us, too. I don't know about your mother but-" The letter was abruptly jerked out of my hands.

"Just stop," Concord snapped coldly. "I've heard enough." I watched as he unpacked his bedding and stalked to the other side of the fire. I knew the anger was directed at his uncle, not me. I was in a daze, the words and phrases swimming around my head meaninglessly. I unrolled my own thin mattress and blanket before settling down, casting one more mournful glance toward the boy across the flames. Closing my eyes, I tried to ignore the shivers to which my body had succumbed.

I jumped when an arm wrapped around me. "I'm sorry," Concord said. As he pulled me closer, warmth washed over me. "Is that better?" he whispered, his breath hitting my neck.

I could only nod in reply. Now that I was warm, sleep began overtaking me. "I'm scared," I confessed drowsily.

"I know, I am too," came his answer. "Go to sleep."

I was almost unconscious when something warm pressed against my forehead. "I promise I'm not going to let anything happen to you. You're all I have left."

The next morning, I awoke with Concord still beside me, reading Nick's letter. Rubbing sleep from my eyes, I rose up next to him. "Morning, Noe," he said. I yawned a reply. Suddenly, he got up. "We should move on. According to this, the hideout is hidden near the base of the mountains. We could reach it today if we leave now."

The thought pained me, but I silently took his outstretched hand and stood. I had never been hiking before and had been shocked when Nick retrieved us from his shop, saying it was already arranged with my parents. If what Nick said was true, they have already been Ordered to forget my existence. I could not think about that now.

I wish I could wake up from this nightmare and return to being a normal teenage girl with normal problems. Instead, I have a computer chip in my head and my government wants me dead because it doesn't work on me. The worst part is that it makes sense. After the Great Wars, the surviving population formed Dimon. Its new government couldn't afford more violence, so the Implant was their solution. Their anti-violence Order worked. War, crime, murder: they are contents of our history books now. I guess the power to control more was too tempting.

By midday we'd made it deep into the forest that surrounded what used to be called the Rockies. Winter had covered the ground with snow that inhaled your boots with each step. I was balanced at the top of a steep ravine, carefully making my way down. I took another step - except my foot kept sliding. "Sh-" I didn't get the word out as gravity threw my body forward, sending me tumbling past Concord and flat on my back at the bottom of the slope. The deep, rumbling laugh I normally adored only caused my face to burn hotter as I pushed myself up.

"N-Noe, ar-are you o-k-kay?" Concord gasped.

"I got to the bottom, didn't I?" I snapped, brushing snow from my clothes. A movement in the shadows caught my attention.

"Look, you made a snow angel." I reached out and grabbed his arm, never taking my eyes from the trees. "Noe, I didn't mean to make fu-"

I cut him off. "Someone's watching us."

He followed my gaze. Fixated, I felt his hand reach behind him and unsheath his knife. I saw the glint of metal before Concord shoved me to the ground just as the gunshot sounded. A loud crack signified its mark on the tree behind us.

A man stepped into view. He was young and dressed in white. A hat concealed his hair; a scarf hid his face except for a pair of thundering gray eyes. Out in the open, his figure blended with the winter landscape. The black gun was trained on Concord. With his free hand, he pulled his scarf down. My eyes immediately jumped to the tattoo on his neck. A red eye with the numbers zero, one, zero written across the pupil and iris. I couldn't tear my gaze from its stare.

"Noemie, you can outrun him. Go," Concord whispered under his breath.

"I'm not leaving you, besides, I'm sick of running," I replied defiantly. His jaw tightened in frustration.

We were interrupted by the man's voice. "I Order you to surrender."

"Not happening, buddy. Unlike you, we're not mindless androids you can Order around," I scoffed.

The man studied us before lowering the gun. He was smiling. "It's nice to have new recruits, and good job finding our hideout."

We looked at him questioningly. He pointed up. I followed his gloved finger and gasped. Above us, high in the forest canopy, was an entire network of bridges and tree-houses that appeared to extend for miles. Lights were beginning to illuminate the treetops and more white figures could be seen emerging from the shadows, watching us, welcoming us.

"The name's Norton," the man said, arms outstretched. "Welcome to the Firewall."

"You used our real names, Perl," Linux said as I finished writing.

"Yeah, Noemie and Concord may be dead for now, but I want us to be ourselves when we look back after this is all over." Closing the book, my eyes trained on the red eye tattooed on my hand.

High School Short Story

Joseph Frost is a twelfth grade student at Roane County High School.

My True Best Friend

I was never a really popular kid throughout my school years. I always tried to keep my head down and focus on the future instead of the now. I never had that many friends or a girlfriend or anything special like most of the kids at my school. My name is Sean by the way, sorry I'm not the best at this sort of stuff, but I'm trying. Even though I wasn't popular or anything, I did always have one friend I could always count on to be there for me through all my problems, and that's where my story starts.

When I was younger, to where I can almost barely remember how old I was, maybe like four or five, I had a very special friend with me, who was imaginary. I didn't know his name at the time, and I really didn't want to be rude and name him because that's not nice to do, you know? Anyway, this friend of mine meant the world to me. We would always go out and have a blast going on "adventures" in my backyard and doing stuff as simple as pretending to be like pirates or something like that (like I said, this was a long, long time ago, so my memory is a little foggy). My friend kept my mind occupied from all the problems that were happening amongst my family, even though I didn't particularly notice them myself being so young.

I was an only child so I didn't really have anyone my age to become good friends with, and even now I still feel that way sometimes. My mom and dad were always busy with their jobs and other activities. I can barely remember times when we would just sit down and talk or play games together as a family, which is why my friend was the closest thing to a brother or close family member I had at the time. Then the big change happened… My parents got into a big fight and split up. I can't particularly remember any details, I just know that I went with my mom, and after that day, I never saw my dad again.

After that event occurred, my mother and I moved away to a different town; a pretty rural area that felt much different than what I was accustomed to. Probably a year or so after that event, stuff more or less turned back to normal. I started up school in this new area. Even though I felt completely alienated from everyone, pretty soon, I started to grow into the school. I even made some new actual friends which made me grow further and further away from the one friend that had been with me through everything.

Middle school was a rather hard time in my life. My mom could barely afford to keep us fed and clothed as well as buy stuff for me I didn't need but wanted. I was young so I never really thought about how much she had truly given to make me happy, even though the stuff she provided me with wasn't nearly as good as my peers' stuff. It makes me sad whenever I look back on it that I didn't say "I love you" or "thank you" as much as I needed to when I was younger. School itself was a challenge for me with those awkward teen years and just feeling like I didn't fit in with any group or anyone. Some of my closest friends who were with me through elementary school had mostly moved away, leaving me alone again ... except for my imaginary friend. Even though I had neglected him and never talked to him, he was always there for me through everything. When I turned back to talk to him, he was there with open arms and open ears.

He had helped through middle school and with practically everything that happened to me during that time, but like I did the first time, I turned away from him again in high school. I started becoming very rebellious to what little family in my mom I had. I started choosing to go hang out with a group of friends who were not, in anyway possible, good for me to be around.

We were always stealing and partying even though I knew I shouldn't be doing it. My grades and life were slowly slipping from me and I didn't do a thing about it. Then one day, this girl came up to me and had started talking with me. I had always seen her around but had never bothered to talk with her or anything like that. I didn't even have any classes with her from what I can recall.

It was such a fortunate day for me. I probably wouldn't have paid any mind to her if I had been with my friends. Lucky for me that I wasn't around any of my friends or people I normally talk to, and she had come up to me from what seemed like nowhere and told me her name. It was Elizabeth, and she had asked me to come to church with her that Sunday. I thought to myself (to figure out if I was doing anything or not) and everyone I could think of had plans for this weekend, so I told her why not and that I would come. Well, Sunday came around and like we said during school, we met up to go to her church. On that day, it changed my life forever. I didn't have the nicest clothes or a Bible or anything like most of the others had. This made me feel really out of place when I first entered the church. Then she took me to where the Sunday School classes were being held. In that classroom everyone was so nice and considerate to me, it made me feel so blessed that I had gone with her.

People I have never seen or talked to before in my age group, they were all so amazing, showed so much compassion to me and made me feel so happy to be there. I was truly happy to be with them and I was so grateful Elizabeth had invited me that day. It was on this day I finally figured out the name of my imaginary friend that had been with me through all the problems I've had throughout my life. All of the difficulties I was faced with, everything I had done to him, I knew why he stayed by me. It was that day that I got saved, and learned that His true name was Jesus Christ. From that day on, my life changed for the better in every way, my best friend was back beside me, and I was devoted to Him forever, as He was devoted to me too. So here I am now, with The Lord by my side, helping me through every step of the way. There's nothing else in the world I would trade for my best friend.

High School Short Story

Emma Jackson is a tenth grade student at Oliver Springs High School.

The Never Ending Love

I was madly in love with my John; he was the glue that held me together through rough times; he was my everything. We had great times. We would laugh and joke with each other; we were just both madly in love. But I never in my right mind thought I would lose my John. We had been married ten years. Everyone thought that we were the cutest couple and that we were going to grow old together and have a big family, especially my mom. We were so in love that everyone around us was jealous. He was the best thing that had ever happened to me. As the years went by our love grew stronger and stronger.

One cold night, me and my John went to a ball at my mother and father's palace. As we arrived, guests were saying hello to me and my John, they were greeting us with their gentleness and kindness. My mother and father held the ball to celebrate me and my John's love for each other because everyone thought we were the perfect match for each other. As we arrived at the ball, my John looked as handsome as ever.

By around midnight we opened presents because if you came to the party you had to bring a gift, so as we came to the last present it had my name on it, so I opened the gift and there was a beautiful diamond necklace wrapped in decorative paper. John took the necklace out and put it around my neck so I could wear it. I wanted to thank whoever got me the necklace because it was the nicest thing anyone had given me besides my ring I got from John. As I looked at the box the necklace came in there was no name or message or anything, it was anonymous. Later that night I told John I wanted to go home because I was getting tired, so we went back to our home in the village and went to bed.

As we were sleeping I rolled over and felt that I was sweating really bad. I woke John up and told him that my neck was burning and that we needed to take my necklace off because it was burning my neck. I didn't take the necklace off when we got home because I was so tired.

John yelled, "I'm going to go get a doctor" and I told him to hurry because I thought I was going to pass out from the pain. We couldn't get the necklace off because when we touched it, it would burn our hands. Ten minutes later John came back with a doctor. The doctor said the necklace had been poisoned, so he got a wet rag and stuck it under the necklace to stop some of the burning, then he told John to go find something to cut the necklace off. John came back with a pair of pliers. John finally started trying to break the necklace and after three tries the necklace broke, and John took it and put it in a bag so that it wouldn't hurt anyone else.

The doctor attended to the wound on my neck and said that it will scar and that I need to keep it from getting infected. We said, "Thank you," and gave him money and he was on his way.

John told me he was glad nothing happened to me because he could not visualize himself without me.

We stayed up all night together thinking who would want to hurt me and why. But then it hit me, who in this whole village can afford a necklace like this one? John said, "Your mom did this," and I said, "I agree," because my mom was really the one who acted strange around me and John like she was jealous or something.

That morning we decided to go to the palace and pay my mother a visit. As we walked to her chamber door we heard her talking to one of the guards, "Is it finished?" The guard said, " Yes, no one was able to remove the necklace, it was burning their hands so I just left."

My mother said, "Good, I was tired of her getting all the attention and having a happy life."

The guard walked away and my mother was finally alone. Me and John snuck into my mother's chambers, and while she had her back turned, before she could turn around, I took the necklace out of the bag and put it around her neck. She turned around and looked at me as if she was innocent and that she had done nothing wrong.

In the end, me and John watched my mother suffer like I did, then she looked at me and said that she was sorry for all the pain she had caused me. So I had John take the necklace off her because I would feel bad for killing my own mother. I told her to give me and John some money and that I never wanted to see her again.

She said, "Ok," and let us leave. Me and my dear John left and never looked back. We used the money my mother gave us to build a house for the big family we had always wanted. We lived the rest of our lives happy and in love.

High School Short Story

Kelvey Nabors is an eleventh grade student who is homeschooled.

The Girl with Purple Hair

It's 3 PM on a Saturday afternoon. The rows of shelves in this bookshop are bathing in the sunbeams like a snake in my grandmother's flowerbeds. On this day, the bookshop had a steady hum of people's hushed voices that reminded me of a hummingbird's flapping wings.

It is through a crack of space between the piles of ragged paperbacks that I see her. A girl with purple hair is standing at the corner of classics and modern literature. I watch her for a moment; she has a demented fear in her actions that pulls me in. Her chipped black nails are shaking to where she can barely hold the book in her hands.

She would hastily peep around the corner then routinely check her phone. It's like her head is a pendulum of a clock ... back and forth her head swings between the corner and the phone like her life depends upon it. Eventually, the phone rings, and those shaking hands hastily turn it on silent, but it's too late! He's found her. A boy with a thunderstorm voice rounds the corner and grips her arm tightly.

She pleads for him to let go. "You're causing a scene," she cries.

But the boy with shiny metal in his face presses closer, and she turns her head away from him, revealing an eye darkened like a moonless night. A spray of cinnamon freckles across her cheeks were like the constellations, and she connects them with the brushing of her hands across the swollen skin. I can't seem to tear my eyes away like a perforated page from the notebook of this sickening sight.

Our eyes connect, hers sending Morse code messages to my little space of the bookshelf.

He's usually not like this, I swear.

I'm gonna break up with him eventually.

I know I don't deserve this, but ...

He says he'll get help if I stay.

It's like a punch in the gut when I realize that in a sick twist of fate or an alternate universe, I could be a girl with purple hair.

I could be the girl with purple hair who hides at the corner of classics and modern literature, gripping *War and Peace* like a lifesaver in a swirling, wind-tossed ocean. I could hide my bruises with makeup and side-swept hair, sending Morse code messages to strangers and making excuses for something that's not my fault.

I lift my unsteady gaze back to hers. I'm taken aback, not expecting the expired look in her eyes. I want to help, but I know it's of no use. She even knows it herself.

It's at this time the tension grows to a boiling point, and the boy grows even more impatient. He shakes her, grabbing a fistful of her long, violet hair in the process. She doesn't cry out, knowing in her gut that if she did it would just make things worse. The tears streaming down her cheeks seal the wax of her bruise and laminates its permanence.

The girl with purple hair is in her own twisted fairytale where there is no ending, happy or tragic. She is in a tower of her own bricklaying. Each brick like a warning that she ignores with mortar, spreading it like excuses over concern. There is no door of escape; only a window of missed opportunities.

She grips his biceps desperately, and I can't help but wonder if those arms ever promised a whole new world. I wonder if his kiss woke her from the coma of normality.

Or maybe the boy with a thunderstorm voice was once the boy with virgin words; maybe his intentions were pure, but the mud of society soiled it.

The thought of innocence lost makes the rain of my own eyes fall. A son's fanciful imaginations transformed into a father's grim reality, and a daughter's fairytale turned into a mother's weeping night.

I return my watery gaze to the smeared oil painting before me and am surprised with a quiet voice.

"I forgive you."

I mirror his look of shock. His face is wiped of the uncontrolled anger and is replaced with haunted apologies.

She dries her tears on his shirt sleeve, and he loosens his grip on her. She kisses the apologies from his skin, and loses herself in hopeful promises.

He quiets the whimpers of her uncertainty with Alcoholics Anonymous. The boy with a thunderstorm voice is now a man with a problem. The girl with purple hair is now a woman with a Head Shrinker. The healing of her skin's bruises is simple, but the damage on her soul is scarring.

She untangles herself from him and moves toward me. She gingerly places her worn copy of *War and Peace* on the shelf in front of my face, and she gives me a knowing smile.

"I won't need this anymore."

Maybe she was right, but I held onto it anyway as a reminder: No one's life is a Disney fairytale.

Middle School Short Story

Mia Janikula is a sixth grade student at Midway Middle School.

The House (edited by Roane Writers Group)

On the end of the street was a tall, ugly, midnight blue house that best friends Sean and Kayla absolutely hated. They seldom even mentioned the structure until one day they decided it might be a good idea to go check out the place. The following night at ten as they walked down the street toward the house they observed the sky was dotted with many stars. As they drew closer they felt as though someone was watching them.

When they reached the front door cold chills ran down the back of their necks. Sean opened the door cautiously and they stepped inside. It was musty-smelling and appeared to have been unoccupied for a long time. They climbed the creaky stairs to the second floor and reached a closed door. Sean's dark blue eyes turned to Kayla with a questioning look. She nodded and they stepped into the room. They immediately felt the urge to lie on the bed and the instant they did they woke up in their own houses, in their own beds!

Kayla didn't remember anything; not even how long she had been asleep. Yet she had an eerie feeling about the last few hours and went downstairs to speak to her mother; ask her if anything strange had happened during the night.

"What do you mean, 'anything strange'?" her mother asked. "You've been upstairs sleeping."

Kayla raced back to her bedroom and called Sean. "Do you remember anything about last night?"

"Kinda," he replied. "I remember going to that creepy house at the end of the street."

Kayla's mom walked in and announced, "You need to get ready for school tomorrow."

The next morning was stormy and gloomy. Everyone at school seemed unusually sad and quiet. Then in class the teacher announced that *Sean Raymond had died late last night*. The whole school was in a panic – no one knew what to do. Kayla and her other best friend Alex started crying. Sean was one of their best friends. They rode the same school bus and Alex lived next door to Kayla. They walked into Kayla's house and told her mother what happened. She started crying because Sean was like a son to her. "We are going down to see Sean's dad," she said.

Later that day they went to see Mr. Raymond but he wasn't home. They decided to go back home and watch the evening news on TV. It said that Mr. Paul Raymond hung himself; everyone was shocked. Both funerals were held on the same day, and everyone was crying.

Later, when Kayla had a dream that she had died, she went downstairs to tell her mother and passed out. She remembers being buried – she was dead.

Elementary School Short Story

Kiyah Love is a fourth grade student at Bowers Elementary School.

The Dog and the Owl

Once upon a time, there was a dog and an owl, they were best, best, best friends for life. But one day the owl wanted a worm to eat, so the dog went to go and try to go and find a worm for the owl to eat.

So when he went into the woods there was this bear, and the bear said, "Ha, come here, Lucas," which is the dog's name.

Bear wanted Lucas to take Owly some worms that he found, and they were in a little jar. Bear gave the jar to Lucas, and Lucas said, "Thanks, Bear."

Lucas ran back to the tree house to give Owly her food. When he got there with the worms, he accidently tripped, and he dropped the jar that was full of worms, but Owly thought that he did that on purpose, but he didn't.

The next day Lucas tried to convince Owly that it was an accident, but she wouldn't budge for a single word that Lucas said. Lucas waited and waited, but one day Lucas got tired of her not treating him with any respect, so he decided to just move on without Owly.

The next day Owly saw Lucas and Bear playing freeze tag with each other, so Owly flew down and asked Lucas, "Can I play too?"

Lucas said no to Owly, so Owly just went back home, and she just watched Lucas and Bear play. Owly was sad and upset, but she knew why Lucas didn't want her to play freeze tag with them.

Here came the next day, so Owly started thinking about Lucas, then Owly just thought to herself, I should go say I'm sorry to Lucas, because Owly missed Lucas so much she just couldn't wait any longer to tell him that she was sorry.

So Owly went to Lucas's house, and she tried to say that she was sorry for being mean to Lucas, so Lucas decided to say that he forgives her. Owly was so happy that they were friends again.

So that next day they all went swimming in Owly's swimming pool, then Bear came looking for Owly so he went in the backyard, and he saw Owly and Lucas swimming. Bear said, "I see you two are friends again," and at the same time they both smiled and said, "Yes, we are."

Elementary School Short Story

Bricen Mee is a fifth grade student at Bowers Elementary School.

The Candy War

In 2020, imagine you are in a war, but not just any war, a candy war. The war began in the dimension of candy. They sent in their best team of candy fighters. There was Bricen the commander, Jeff the healer, Adam the guns, and Michael the support.

The team went to the candy dimension. The mission was to get the ultimate sun battle hammer to defeat the Samurai master. The Samurai master commands the candy army.

Bricen begins to go to the ultimate battle hammer statue. On the way there, he ran into candy alien troops and there were too many for him to defeat. He escaped and went back to camp. The next day his team went with him to find the candy alien troops. This time, they defeated the troops, and they got the ultimate sun battle hammer.

They start to head to the candy castle. They had to eat through the candy door to enter the castle. They battled the candy dragon with chocolate armor. They melted the chocolate armor, and the dragon ran away embarrassed.

Boom! Boom! Two doors open, and the Samurai master runs in the courtyard and the battle begins again. It was rough, but the team won the battle. We all did the wip na na in excitement when we took over the candy castle.

High School Poetry

Ethan Burnett is a tenth grade student at Oliver Springs High School.

A Strife with the Unknown

For the many things that darkness can conceal,

the absence of thought is the worst ideal.

We are no longer rational to perceive what we feel.

So instead we dwell on the sensation of zeal.

A few are flawed, while others are factual.

So we weave our reason together,

to appear as if they were actual.

Even if some stay in a quarrel,

hopefully most won't erupt in turmoil.

To grasp comprehension is truly absurd.

Knowledge always acts as if it were heard.

Whether concealed in the distance or under our nose,

It tends to use our blind ambitions as roads.

No one knows where this façade will go.

There is only one thing assured.

No one can genuinely know.

High School Poetry

Kelvey Nabors is an eleventh grade student who is home schooled.

The Boy with a Thunderstorm Voice

Once upon a time there was a Dragon,

A Prince as his disguise.

Flowers, dates, and chocolate,

They mesmerized.

But the Prince lost his job, and his palace was evicted.

So he became the boy with a thunderstorm voice,

And a bottle he was inflicted.

He grips the arms of innocence.

The scars on her face tell his story;

The bruises a symbol of reliance.

Then the thunder ceased and quiet commenced.

She begged for peace; he kept her from jumping the fence.

A kiss of deception, "Therapy is the answer."

An embrace of corruption and abuse,

A few Morse code messages through a flat expression,

"What's the use?"

High School Poetry

Reves Schaefer is a ninth grade student who is home schooled.

Sisters

They giggle and laugh

They talk and they play,

They smile and sing

As they go through their day.

With my sisters, I am never bored

For my sisters, I thank you, Lord.

They challenge and encourage me

To be the man God wants me to be.

Yes, these are my sisters

My very best friends

They are there for me

Whether I lose or win.

Yes, these are my sisters

A gift from above

Heaven sent treasures

From the Lord, with love.

High School Poetry

Kallie Sohm is a twelfth grade student at Midway High School.

Lost in the Pages

Fiction and my reality are burled

Who knows what is real anyway?

This place couldn't be my world

In my nursery, I found a boy's shadow unfurled

In return he introduced me to mermaids on a faraway cay

Fiction and my reality are burled

Wearing beautiful gowns with my hair curled,

I danced with Mr. Darcy on the grounds of Pemberley

So, this place couldn't be my world

I met a caterpillar once, whose hooka smoke was twirled,

Into all the words that he would say

Fiction and my reality are burled

I've spoken to the ghost of Cathy as she knitted and purled

Heathcliff simply grumbled in his usual way

So, this place couldn't be my world

Every time I read a page I'm whirled,

Off to a place where I can play

Fiction and my reality are burled

This place couldn't be my world.

Middle School Poetry

Dalton Bacon is a sixth grade student at Midway Middle School.

Names

They are always over used

And sometimes even can be abused

Some are bold and

Some are small

But in the end they define us all

This is true

We all knew

It has happened to us all

Don't feel bad it's happened to me too

They think it's funny

They think it's cute

But it's really not

No matter what.

Middle School Poetry

Jacob Gardner is a sixth grade student at Midway Middle School.

Gym Class

Gym class is fun

but we have to run

it's not so fun

when we are done

we have to lift weights

but someone's not strong

he can't even do it five times long

when we play dodgeball

we all start to call

he can't even throw

or make the ball go

he can't shoot

we all think it is a hoot

and he kinda smells like a boot

Middle School Poetry

Aubrey Walden is a sixth grade student at Midway Middle School.

Leap of Leopards

The other day

I saw a leap of leopards,

They were sitting by a tree.

And a troop of kangaroos

came hopping free.

There was a brood of hens

I could see from afar,

And a pride of lions

chasing a car.

I saw a school of fish

swimming in a lake,

And a gaggle of geese

eating a cheese cake.

I saw a band of gorillas

running by the sea,

and a yoke of oxen

chasing after me.

I fled into a herd of cows

munching on grass,

Their eyes look to ask

if I will join,

But this time,

I think I will pass.

Middle School Essay

Marlena Alexander is an eighth grade student at Cherokee Middle School.

The Death of Edgar Allan Poe

Edgar Allan Poe was an eighteenth century poet who wrote many mysterious poems. By age twenty-one, he had already published two volumes of poetry, and his success continued until the year 1849. All good things must end, and on October 7, 1849, Edgar Allan Poe mysteriously departed from this earth, just like a character from one of his poems.

The cause of Poe's death has yet to be confirmed. I believe through my research, Edgar Allan Poe died of a natural occurring brain tumor induced by alcoholism, caused by cooping. According to smithsonian.com, when Poe died he was buried rather ordinarily in an unmarked grave in Baltimore Graveyard. Poe's coffin was dug up two decades later, and his skeleton was exhumed.

Little remained of Poe's body but one worker was able to find a mass rolling inside his head. Smithsonian.com stated that, "Matthew Pearl, an American author who wrote a novel about Poe's death, was interested in this clump. He contacted a forensic pathologist who told him the clump could not be his brain, but could have easily been a brain tumor which usually calcifies after death into a hard mass."

There was an election on the day Poe was found. Wikipedia says, "Baltimore was known as a mob-town." The elections were also known to be extremely violent. During one of these elections one might be cooped, which refers to an unwilling participant who was forced to vote, often several times, for a particular candidate in the election.

When Poe was found, he was delirious and possibly intoxicated. When you were cooped, the person would often give you alcohol so that you would be easily persuaded to do their bidding. The people who cooped Poe most likely did not know about his allergy to alcohol. Given in great amounts, with Poe's allergy, a brain tumor could form. As Smithsonian.com plainly states "A New York doctor had once told Poe he had a lesion on his brain caused by adverse reactions to alcohol."

Gas lighting is another possible theory for the death of Poe. As Smithsonian.com stated, "In 1999 Public Health researcher, Albert Donnay argued a that Poe's death was the result of carbon monoxide poisoning from coal gas that was used for indoor lighting in the nineteenth century." Donnay took clippings of Poe's hair and tested it for heavy metals that would be able to reveal the presence of coal gasses." The weakness is that the test came back inconclusive, leaving biographers and historians to highly discredit Donnay's theory.

As I have shown you in my writing above, the most logical explanation of Edgar AllanPoe's death is a brain tumor caused by alcoholism, during cooping.

Lo! Death had rear'd himself a throne

in a strange city, all alone

Far down within the dim west -

Where the good, the bad, the worst and best

Have gone to their eternal rest

~Edgar Alan Poe

Middle School Essay

Tayler Bonafede is an eighth grade student at Midway Middle School.

Social Media

Every day, social media is changing the world around us. The effects of social media can be very powerful. Some people use social media for communicating with family or friends a long distance away. One of the most popular ways of making these connections is through the popular networking site Facebook.

Most people use Facebook as a way of communicating with friends or relatives they haven't seen in a while or don't live close to in distance. Many times, people use it to find relatives they have never met or they use it to track down family members who may be missing and they fear something may have happened to them.

Facebook allows you the choice to choose to "friend" someone or not to do so if you are unsure of who they are. You can decline their invitation and request to not receive notifications from that person again. This can be a helpful feature to keep you from being the victim of harassment.

Facebook has many groups you can join depending on your interests. There is something for almost every age group. If you are interested in certain sports and athletes, you can join fan pages for those groups. If you are interested in certain hobbies or enjoy certain types of music, you can join groups relating to those things.

Sometimes people who are starting new jobs or new businesses will use Facebook as a way to get the word out to people they may know living in a certain area. That information is then passed on to other people who may be friends of their friends. This may help their business get off to a much better start than it would have.

Facebook also has a news feed so that you can view news updates while you are on the home page so that you are up to date on major things that have happened during the day while you may have been at work or at school.

For those who enjoy playing games online but don't like games offered on certain other web pages, Facebook has specific games that are only played on Facebook. You can create your own virtual worlds. You can create everything from farming towns to sorority characters. There are a variety of trivia games that can be played to test your knowledge of the world.

With this being an election year, social media like Facebook is sometimes used by people running for office to give them an idea of how well they are doing in the polls and why people may or may not vote for them. It gives them an idea of which groups of people support them so that they may get elected for office.

Unfortunately, Facebook isn't always used in ways it is intended. There have been false accounts created using other people's pictures. Sometimes people are bullied by people that they go to school with who may spread rumors about them and see this as the fastest way of bothering that person. They may do this because they know that schools can't stop this type of bullying since it is usually done outside of school hours and schools can't tell students how to use their free time away from school. You just have to let the good parts of Facebook be more important to you than the bad parts.

Another form of social media that is becoming very popular is Instagram. Instagram is different from Facebook in that is uses mostly pictures and video as a way of communicating with others. Instagram has more safety features than other sites like Snapchat and Twitter. It uses a private account where users can request to see your pictures and videos. If you don't know the person wanting to see your pictures or videos, you can decline their request.

Another feature is advertisements. You can see advertisements for movies and other social networking sites. Instagram can provide you with a list of people that you may want to follow and keep up with their pictures and videos. You can link websites that may be important to you through Instagram. For example, if you have your own YouTube page, you can place this as a link on your Instagram page.

Unfortunately, just like Facebook, there hasn't been a way created yet when you use Instagram to keep someone from hacking into your account or taking an opportunity to bully someone they may not like. It is simply a matter of being responsible and respectful.

In conclusion, the goal of social media is to help those using it and not to harm them. It is designed to be a link to those we may not see every day. It is not meant to be a replacement for real human contact, but it is a very close second in the real world as we know it today.

Middle School Essay

Rebekah Brooks is an eighth grade student at Midway Middle School.

The Wonderful World of Lucid Dreaming

Have you ever in your life heard of lucid dreaming? Do you know what this wonderful process is? Lucid dreaming is when you are lucid, awake, or in control, while dreaming. The wonderful process of lucid dreaming allows you to control your dreams. How do you induce lucid dreaming? Lucid dreaming can be induced by different ways, but you can also use music, alarms, or other things to help you. If you do use this to help you, make sure you are no awaken up by these or you will have to restart this process. There are also many benefits to this wonderful process.

If you haven't heard of lucid dreaming, then I feel very sorry for you. Lucid dreaming is when you are lucid or awake, while your body is asleep or dreaming. Complicated, right? Actually, it is not that hard to wrap your mind around. Basically, your brain never rests, but the rest of your body does, in fact, sleep. Therefore, it is possible for your brain to be fully awake while the rest of your body is completely asleep. So, how do you tap into the wonderful process of lucid dreaming?

The amazing process of lucid dreaming can be induced in many different ways. Most of these take a while; some will work for you and some will not work for you. The point of all this is, all of the various plans differ, and it can take quite a while for you to learn. For example, it took me three very hard months, and to this day it still takes a lot of effort for me when attempting to lucid dream. One of the methods is called WILD, which an acronym meaning wake induced lucid dreaming. In this theory, you induce lucid dreaming by lying spread out on a surface, typically your bed, while being perfectly still and quiet and breathe in and out slowly. The key to this exercise is for your body and your mind to relax. By doing this, your brain will reach the REM stage more quickly. REM stands for rapid eye movement, and this is also the point when your body begins to dream. All of this is great, but what do you do when you begin to dream?

Once you start to drift off, close your eyes and repeat this phrase internally, "You are dreaming, you are dreaming, you are dreaming," and then passively think about what you would like to dream of that night. You can use stimulating music or an alarm to help with this stage, but be careful because this can awaken you and you will have to start this process all over again. If you do choose to use this method, record a song or audio of yourself or someone else speaking, set a timer for about an hour because this is about how long it will take you to access the REM stage of sleep again. The audio of your voice should say, "You are dreaming," over and over again in a deep, soft voice. Now, how exactly do you control your dreams?

Well, when you are sleeping, if you have followed my above directions, and gave it some time, you should be a fully lucid dreamer. All you should have to do is think about what you want to dream about that night. These dreams can be about anything you can imagine, from flying to your normal, everyday life. There is only one problem with this, though. If you cannot imagine it, you cannot dream it. Therefore, you must have an imagination to have any variety in your lucid dreams. To have some variety, I suggest you listen to alternative music or try new things because this process is both mental and physical.

In conclusion, lucid dreaming is a wonderful process. Lucid dreaming is when your mind is awake and all of your physical body is asleep. Because your mind is lucid, your mind can control your dreams. All of this is great, but how can lucid dreaming be induced? You can use many different methods to induce this wonderful process, but I prefer WILD. WILD is the acronym for wake induced lucid dreaming. You can induce this process by lying still and breathing in and out slowly, and then waiting for the rapid eye movement stage to occur. Lastly, just take control of your mind. You can use many different methods to help with this, including music or alarms, but be careful not to get awakened again, because you will have to restart this amazing, yet long process. Having an imagination also helps to have a lot more variety in your lucid dreams whenever you have them, because you can dream of more. Last, you just have to dream.

Middle School Essay

Sarah Collins is an eighth grade student at Midway Middle School.

Child Abuse and Adoption

Have you ever wondered what it was like to know someone who was abused as a child? Well it's not easy to know someone has or is being abused. When a child is born, they could start getting abused by their parents, no matter how old they are. It's not easy for a child to go through their life getting abused, so that they end up getting adopted. When a child gets adopted, they have to start a new life. They have to meet their new parents and family members. Also, they have to forget the friends that they use to know. Going through adoption is much harder than you think.

When a child gets adopted, they have to leave their friends behind and try to make new ones. It's not easy when a child has to move to a new neighborhood and school. Also, it can be very hard when their new parents want to talk about the past to them. Knowing that, adopted kids might actually want to share their feelings to someone very close to them. For example: their parents, a close friend, or maybe even one of their family members. But don't forget about why kids have to get adopted.

The majority of the time, kids are getting abused by their parents. Child abuse can lead to many problems. For example: When kids get punished for no good reason. Also, some kids don't even get freedom like other kids do. It's sad because some parents keep their kids locked up inside their house the whole time. Also, when a kid is getting abused, they can be afraid to tell anyone. The reason is because, they could lose the people they care about. The majority of the time brothers and sisters get separated during the adoption process. I think that child abuse should come to an end.

When I think about child abuse, I think that the people who hurt kids should get punished for it. It can be extremely hard for children who get abused. Kids don't deserve to get abused just because their parents aren't happy with themselves. A lot of kids that are in this situation handle it in many different ways. For example: some kids might even have nightmares because they're getting abused. Others might take it to extreme. It's just awful to know that parents would abuse their own children. The kids who are getting abused don't even know why they have to go through this.

Did you ever think about what really went on in an abused family? Well, when kids start to get abused, they might not even get to go to school and get an education. Some abused kids might end up with a learning disability. Others might get held back, since they were never provided the education they needed. But one thing an abused kid would pray for was to have a new family. Some kids would stay up late and wonder what it would be like to have a new family.

If you could take a moment, and think about what it was like to be and abused child, would you? To know what they went through and how they dealt with it. It wouldn't be really be easy. See, that's how hard it can be for an abused child. They don't know who to tell or how to explain their feelings. Some kids might get lost in how they feel and how they wish that they didn't get abused. It can be very hard to understand what an abused kid has gone through.

Many people might at least know somebody who has been through child abuse or maybe you experienced it yourself too. I know how difficult child abuse can be because even I know someone who's been through this situation. And to tell you the truth, an abused kid just needs someone close to them to know that they would always be there for them. Also, knowing that child abuse can lead to adoption, doesn't mean it's going to be easy. Knowing that kids have a hard time trying to figure out who they are, they will soon figure out who their going to be. So, next time you know an adopted kid, stop and try to be in their shoes for once, to know how they feel.

Middle School Essay

Lucas Goldschmidt is an eighth grade student at Midway Middle School.

The Importance of Music

Music has a lot of impact on the listener. It can change their mood or life entirely. A type of music you listen to might define who you are. Music might also have a huge impact if you play. You might play music because you have a personal connection, or just enjoy it. I play because it gives me the sense I have accomplished something.

Music can build character in many different ways. It can provide you with natural rhythm. Music can also help with sleight of hand as well. It can also give you skills, depending on what you play, like finger skills etc. Overall though, it gives you concentration. This can help with everyday life things like school. Music can calm you in a stressful situation. It can also help you through difficult times.

Music also has many genres. What genre you like might depend on what kind of person you are. Music like Metallica, Iron Maiden, etc. have personally helped me. Music in this genre is deep but yet still exciting. Playing this type of music has an even bigger impact. Playing this music gives me a sense of accomplishment. In this I am challenged but also excited.

The music you listen to also depends on what you play, or vice versa. A violinist might be partial to classical music, while an electric guitar player might like Metal/Rock. This also might depend on your personality. For instance, a shy person might like to play the flute, while a sporadic person might like the drums.

In conclusion, music has a lot of impact on the listener. It can help through difficult times. It can also change or build character. Music may also help with concentration. The music someone likes might depend on their personality.

Middle School Essay

Dequin Kile is an eighth grade student at Midway Middle School.

Chris Kyle

Chris Kyle was America's most lethal military sniper. Kyle was called "The Legend" by his colleges. Kyle earned 160 kills in his career, making Kyle the most lethal sniper in U.S. Military history. Kyle served his country for 10 years, serving in four deployments.

Kyle was born on April 8, 1974, in Odessa, Texas. Kyle's father, a church deacon, taught him the importance of freedom and to respect and appreciate what he has. This shaped Kyle into the man he was. Kyle enjoyed hunting deer and pheasant.

Later in Kyle's life, the cowboy in him kicked in. Kyle competed in a number of bronco busting contests. One time, while getting on the enraged bronco, it flipped over on top of Kyle in the chute in Rendon, Texas. The guys watching could not open the chute because of the way the horse fell. So they had to pull the horse back over him. Kyle was kicked so hard he lost consciousness. Kyle had to have pins put into his wrist and had a dislocated shoulder, broken ribs, and a bruised lung and kidney. That ended Kyle's bronco busting career.

Looking for some extra cash, Kyle worked at a lumber yard delivering wood and other materials. One day a guy asked Kyle if he wanted to work for a friend of his as a ranch hand. Kyle excitedly accepted the job. Kyle went to work for David Landrum in Hood county Texas. Landrum taught Kyle more than he thought he knew about ranching. Kyle described Landrum as a tough, hardworking man.

Kyle loved being on the ranch. Kyle enjoyed working with animals all day and being outside. Kyle liked the idea of being alone and working without the disturbance of crowded offices. Kyle had many responsibilities on the ranch, so Landrum bumped his salary up to 400 dollars a month. This is where Kyle learned one of his most important skills that helped him in the military: patience. Kyle cut horses to get them ready for auction. Once trained, the horses could help cowboys cut cows from herds. "If you were not patient with a horse, you could ruin it for life," Kyle once said. Kyle also learned to stay confident in himself, and that played a major role in becoming a SEAL.

One day in 1996, Kyle had made up his mind at what he wanted to do with his life. He went to a recruiting station. He first wanted to join the Marines, but the recruiter was out at lunch. As Kyle started out the door, the recruiter from the Army hollered and said, "Come over here." The recruiter asked Kyle, "What are you interested in?"

Kyle responded, "The SF" (Special Forces). The recruiter told him that he had to be an E5 (a sergeant) to be in the SF. The recruiter told Kyle about the Army Rangers. Kyle liked the idea of jumping out of plains and assaulting the enemy. Kyle told the recruiter he would think about the idea. As Kyle was walking out of the building, the Navy recruiter called him over to his desk. The recruiter asked Kyle, "What were you talking about?"

Kyle replied, "We were talking about the SF, but you have to be an E5 to join." The recruiter then told Kyle about the SEALs. Kyle liked the idea of a hard challenge physically and mentally. Kyle was informed that only ten percent make it through the training. Kyle left thinking about what to do. Kyle decided that he would join the Navy SEALs. Kyle was told that the Navy couldn't promise that he would be a SEAL, but they told him they would give him a chance to fail anyway. Kyle accepted the challenge. So he went back to the recruiting station to sign the papers but was turned down because of the pins in his wrist. Kyle pleaded with them, even trying to tell them he would not hold the Navy responsible for anything that happened to his wrist, but they still said no.

Kyle thought that would be the end of his military career. Between the years 1997 and 1998, Kyle had decided to make a career in ranching. Kyle was working in Colorado while planning to come back to Texas and work for Landrum when he got a phone call. Kyle was in the beginning stages of becoming a SEAL. Kyle fought through BUD/S (Basic Underwater Demolition). Kyle loved every bit of it even though they were being beat down, spit on, and chewed up and spit out.

It took Kyle a better part of the year to complete BUD/S. He joined the Navy and went to basic training in February 1999. Kyle thought that basic training was too easy. At one point, Kyle called his dad and told him that ranch work was a lot harder than basic training. When Kyle graduated BUD/S, he was in top physical condition. Kyle and his peers were challenged to their max. Kyle had all sorts of things that kept him motivated. One was remembering all the people who told him that he would flunk. Kyle was determined to prove them wrong.

Becoming a Navy SEAL takes more mental toughness than physical. Kyle had to fight through one of the toughest weeks in BUD/S: Hell Week. Hell Week is a five day long course of highly intense exercise. This is where most candidates fail and drop out. Kyle was one of the twenty-four men to make it through. After Kyle had pulled through Hell Week, he started to build a friendship with Marcus Luttrell. Both being from Texas and having the same interests and toughing out BUD/S, they got along pretty well. Kyle and Luttrell kept in touch over the years.

Kyle was now a SEAL, but he didn't consider himself a SEAL until he was on a SEAL team and had proven to the team that he was worthy enough to join the team. Kyle had a choice of six teams. Kyle's top choice was Team Three because they had seen action in the Middle East and were likely to return. Kyle got his top choice. Kyle was now an official member of a SEAL team.

Something else also happened to Kyle that summer. He met Taya, his future wife. Things were going well for Kyle, he had just joined a SEAL team and had a week for vacation and had met the girl of his dreams. Taya and Kyle were starting to get along better and staying the night at each other's apartments. On the morning of September 11, 2001, Kyle woke up to Taya screaming, "Wake up, Chris! Chris, wake up!"

Kyle walked into the living room to see Nine Eleven unfold on his television. Kyle was ordered to report to base immediately. Ready to see action, Kyle rushed to the base. It turned out that his team wouldn't see action until a year later to fight Saddam Hussein, not Osama bin Laden. Kyle and his team began to train in all conditions. The word was out that the best trained team would be deployed. It was a competition with Kyle's team coming in second. Kyle's team had to stay home.

Later Kyle's team was deployed to a Naval ship. Kyle was awakened and told, "We got a tanker," one of the helicopters had spotted an oil tanker trying to sneak down the Gulf after loading up illegally in Iraq. The mission was to board, inspect papers, and if it was violating U.N. sanctions, turn it over to the Marines or other authorities. That was Kyle's first mission as a SEAL. It wasn't until later in his career that he would be a sniper.

While on vacation after the first deployment, Kyle decided to end his vacation short and attend a sniper school. The school was one of the hardest schools to pass next to BUD/S, according to Kyle. Only fifty percent made it through the school. Kyle used a range of four sniper rifles, depending on the type of situation. Kyle used the Mk-12, Mk-11, .300 Win Mag, and a .50 Caliber. Kyle was serving with the GROM, a Polish Special Force when he got his first chance at sniping. Kyle was sent to Fallujah. Kyle would be assigned over watch for the Marines that were planning to make a big push. Kyle jumped on the opportunity, eager to see action. Kyle and a friend from BUD/S, Ray, took turns taking over watch for the Marines.

Kyle continued to keep up his reputation. The Marines trusted Kyle with their lives more than anybody else. Unfortunately on February 2, 2013, Chris Kyle was murdered by an ex-Marine. Kyle was awarded two Silver Stars, five Bronze Stars with Valor, and numerous other citations. Kyle believed highly in our nation and what we stand for. Kyle was a true American hero.

Middle School Essay

April Lance is a seventh grade student at Midway Middle School.

Scotty McCreery

Twenty-two-year-old country star Scotty McCreery has made it big after winning the tenth season of American Idol. He has reached out and touched many people's hearts throughout America. Most people have fell in love with his amazing deep voice and country accent, but Scotty also has other sides than just singing.

Scotty was born and raised in Garner, North Carolina, on October 9, 1993. His parents Michael and Judy originally planned on naming him Evan but changed their minds on the day of the delivery. Scotty is a quarter Puerto Rican from his father's side. When he was just one-year-old, he begun humming tunes, but it took a while for a deep voice to appear. Scotty began taking guitar lessons at the age of nine and showed his musical promise with his natural rhythm, which has always came relatively easily to him – proving that true talent shows no age limit. He attended Timber Drive Elementary School, West Lake Middle School, and Garner Magnet High School. When Scotty was still at Timber Drive Elementary School, he put on concerts on the back of the bus. Brett Bailey, Scotty's longtime friend, says, "He started singing Elvis on the back of the bus. It was almost like a mini Elvis concert."

Scotty's father played baseball, and his mother's distant cousin was a professional player. Scotty's family all enjoys playing baseball and so does Scotty. If Scotty hadn't made it in music, he could have fallen back to baseball as a career. Because of his love for baseball, he used a flute-like microphone grip in the early rounds of American Idol.

Scotty's idol is Josh Turner. Scotty says, "One thing I love about Josh Turner is his faith. That is why I looked up to him so much. All the albums he has had have at least one Christian song, like The Answer on his last album and Long Black Train. So I'm hoping to have that on my album, that one Christian song.

Scotty is a good Christian man. He seems to inject his Christian faith into every aspect of his life. He was raised Southern Baptist, in a First Baptist Church in Garner. Scotty loves Jesus Christ with all his heart and credits Jesus for both his voice and getting him through American Idol. Scotty has said he requires any future girlfriend or wife to be a Christian. The cross around Scotty's neck, which is just a symbol of his faith, became more famous than the word around his wrist which says, "I am second," meaning that God is first.

At seventeen, Scotty became the youngest male to win American Idol during the tenth season. Scotty's first album, *Clear as Day*, came out when he was seventeen years old and was certified platinum in the United States. He also had a Christmas album right after that. His second album, *See You Tonight*, came when he was nineteen years old, and now at twenty-two, he has his third album, *Southern Belle*. Scotty says he hears that he is too young and what does he have to sing about? Scotty says, "Well, in case you didn't know, I'm leaving out a lot of stuff."

Scotty says, "God gave me a voice and America gave me a chance." That's one of the things he is writing about in his new book, *Go Big or Go Home: The Journey Toward the Dream*. Scotty worked on his new album *Southern Belle* and his book this summer, which took up most of his time.

Arriving May 3, 2016, Scotty McCreery's new book *Go Big or Go Home: The Journey Toward the Dream* is set to come out, which will narrate Scotty's journey from childhood imitations of Elvis riding the school bus to winning the tenth season of American Idol and then building a successful career in the country genre. Scotty says that in the book, "We're telling stories about my life so I guess it's an autobiography, but I call it a travelogue because it's my experience and perspective. I had to grow up at sixteen, so my perspective at twenty-two is different from other twenty-two-year-old boys just now meeting the world."

Scotty's life has been adventurous. He has had his ups and downs, but God has pulled him through. He's made it far in country music and now has written a book. Hopefully he'll do even more and make it further in country music. He is or will be one day an idol to another young boy.

Middle School Essay

Kadie Lewis is an eighth grade student at Midway Middle School.

Print and Pixels: A Guide to Books

Many people have been debating whether or not paper books or digital books are better. Are digital books missing a certain something that makes people want to read? Or are paper books overpriced and unnecessary due to growing technology? Some people may say it doesn't matter. A book is a book whether in print or pixels. To decide this, people can look to the past and the pros and cons of both printed books and e-books. Analyzing both e-books and print books, can help people decide which is better.

A History of Printed Books and Electronic Books:

To get a better view, you can look to the past. Printed books in 2400 BC weren't books at all but papyrus scrolls. From that time papyrus scrolls had made the slow but sure evolution into printed, bound books. Not until around 610 AD did paper-making finally make an entrance. Papermaking was first introduced into Japan from China. After that, paper-making started spreading like wildfire through Asia and finally Europe. Now that paper was established, you needed print. In 1500, printing was established in more than two hundred fifty European cities.

Electronic books, or e-books, have a more recent past. In 1968, Alan Kay introduced the Dynabook. From the Dynabook, Alan Kay envisioned the day when libraries could be portable. His vision led to today's laptops. Finally, in 1971, Michael Hart established Gutenberg. Around 1996, project Gutenberg reached 1000 e-texts. In 2007, Amazon launched kindles and went out of stock in five hours. In the same year, CourseSmart was founded and provided e-textbooks for students' learning in higher education, and the Kindle was featured on the cover of Newsweek's November issue. In 2010, Amazon e-books outpaced hardcover sales for the first time.

The Pros and Cons of Printed Books and E-books:

Another way you can decide is looking at the pros and cons of printed books. There're many pros and cons of printed books. Printed books make reading physically enjoyable by their nice soft pages. Printed books are physical proof of your intellectual journeys. Your beat up copies of novels can remind you of your times in high school or other parts of your life. Print books are also better for your health. A recent study at Harvard Medical School found that lit up e-books could interfere with your ability to sleep. And since your sleep is a key factor in your health, it may affect your overall health. However, with every positive, there are negatives. Printed books can be cumbersome to handle, making them less portable than e-books. Price and necessity are also some cons. New and rare releases can have quite the price. Others may be unavailable in some areas.

E-books also have some pros and cons that need to be weighed in the balance before making decision. E-books are lighter, multi-taskable, and have a bounty of online resources. This makes e-books more portable and user-friendly. Not only can you read almost anywhere, you can read almost anything anywhere. Nevertheless, there are also cons to e- books. E-books can run out of battery life, making your whole book disappear. Also dropping one of your e-readers can result in the destruction of an entire library.

Why choosing Printed Book or E-books Matters:

So, why does it matter? Whether you read e-books or print books, reading is reading. Reading is important for many more reasons than entertainment. Reading can help people stay mentally stimulated. By keeping your brain active, you stop your brainpower from diminishing in upcoming years. Reading can also help stress. Losing yourself in a good book helps to veil your issues in the real world. So, let your woes slip away while you slip into a good book. Knowledge and vocabulary expansion might be the most well-known, however. Everything you read adds to your store of information and can make you better equipped in the particular situations the information relates to. Also, the more you read the more exposure you gain to higher words. Being articulate can help you in any profession.

Memory improvement, stronger analytic thinking skills, improved concentration, and better writing skills are all the more ways that reading is beneficial. When reading, it is vitally important to remember needed information in order to gain the proper reading experience. By analyzing the book, you learn to analyze real-world situations. For the few who have problems or just have straying thoughts, books can help you learn to focus. When you read a book your whole, undivided attention is key when trying to enjoy a book. Moreover, writing skills is another skill that comes with reading. During reading, your brain is constantly analyzing every detail that goes towards the plot. You will find during writing you will utilize well-written technique you come across, while discarding every unskillful technique you read. Readers can find all these benefiting factors no matter whether you decide to read in pixels or print.

In conclusion, when reading books you have two options: e-books or print books. The e-book and the print book are great ways to enjoy the benefits of reading. Looking at the history and the pros and cons of both the e-reader and traditional print books can help you decide. However, you may say it doesn't matter; after all, a book is a book. Even so, reading is a great way to improve, help, and keep your brain in tip-top condition. Whether you read in pixels or print, reading is always a great choice to make

Middle School Essay

Alex Limburg is an eighth grade student at Midway Middle School.

Service Dog Benefits

Many people in this generation have disabilities. These disabilities can be mental or physical. Yet, many people don't realize they can help the people with disabilities by providing service dogs or animals. Service dogs are a great way to show support and relieve stress. There is also a financial benefit in this situation. Service dogs are very caring and provide much needed emotional support.

People with mental disabilities such as autism and other conditions might require a service dog. For instance, hypersomnia is an illness that makes it hard to stay awake during the day. People who have hypersomnia can fall asleep at any time. The service dog would be responsible for waking up the owner or alerting someone else of the mishappening. Memory loss is also a symptom that, in some cases, would be beneficial to have a service dog. The service dog would need to remind the person of medication, find lost items, and help perform routine prompts, such as getting dressed as well as taking a shower.

Mood swings in some cases also would benefit from a service dog. A mood swing is an abrupt and apparently, unaccountable change of moods. Mood swings can be very dangerous to the safety of people. The dog would be alert to such changes in behavior. Sometimes the dog would serve as a distraction to calm down the owner. Post-Traumatic Stress Disorder (PTSD) is a great example of mood swings. PTSD is an illness that someone acquires after they have been through a devastating experience. The majority of the people that get it are military veterans. These veterans react to noises and scenery that trigger memories of what they experienced on the battlefield. These victims of war would use a service dog to deal with stress or cope over a fallen friend.

People die every day. The people who die in a horrible way usually have family members that grieve their loss. That family can become very depressed and some of them develop anxiety. My brother was in a car accident and had a traumatic brain injury and he went into a coma. The damage to his brain caused him not to be able to recover, and he died. When I heard the news, I didn't cry. I felt absolutely emotionless. At times, I have anxiety about certain situations or when I am thinking about Josh. I have a dog, but he is not a service dog. Yet, even though he is not a service dog, he still helps me calm down when I think of my brother. These are just a few of the mental disabilities that people suffer and why people need service dogs in their lives.

There are many physical needs for a service dog too. Diabetes, cancer and the list goes on and on. People with diabetes can benefit from service dogs. The reason is if their blood sugar gets too low, the dog will alert them to eat food that will bring their blood sugar up. Cancer can be very depressing and can be devastating to an individual and their family. Dogs bring happiness. Cancer is bad, and as we are looking for cures to cancer, we can use dogs to decrease the depressive symptoms people have. Service dogs can help to alleviate depressive symptoms and help to alert diabetics of their physical symptoms to help them cope with their illness. These are two examples of how service dogs can help in medical diagnoses.

Seizures are very dangerous to any person. A seizure is basically a heart attack in the brain. When a seizure occurs, your body immediately starts shaking and the victim becomes unresponsive. My brother, Noah, had a seizure while he was driving. His friend at the time was able to stop the vehicle and save him. After the accident, my brother had smaller seizures that didn't affect him as bad. Every time he had a smaller seizure, his dog would try to comfort him.

Many people purchase fake items for their dogs. These items consist of fake vests, IDs, and other things that identify an animal as a service dog. These kinds of people don't understand the real need for these dogs.

A study conducted in 1996 shows that there is a financial benefit to owning a service dog. The reason for this is some families pay a lot for other people to come and see if something is wrong and to assist with the person daily or sometimes weekly. A service dog can detect something is wrong immediately and alert others to help the patient. The total saving amount is $13,000 for every year. By saving all this money over the years, people could use the money to help their children or other family members.

In conclusion, many people don't realize all of the benefits of owning a service dog. If people would do their research, they would find all of the amazing things, such as happiness, companionship, and many other benefits. It is important to consider all of the benefits about everything that these amazing dogs do. People should also acknowledge that people might lie about their dog being a service dog, which is a heinous act. Even though not all of the benefits of owning a service dog are listed, a lot of the same principles apply. People need these dogs in their lives.

Middle School Essay

Alysan Limburg is a seventh grade student at Midway Middle School.

Siberian Husky

Siberian Huskies are known for helping mankind. The breed is believed to come from the tribe Chukchi of Siberia. Siberian Huskies were used for many different reasons like herding reindeer, pulling sleds and keeping children warm. This breed has been famous since 1925.

Some cool facts about Siberian Huskies are that they were used during World War II as search and rescue dogs and also used for transportation and communication. They are also very close relatives to the Grey Wolf, like the shiba inu and chow chow dog breeds. Huskies are the only dog breed to have blue eyes naturally. Other breeds can have blue eyes, but that is because of a gene that makes their eyes have no pigment, which makes them blue.

Siberian Huskies are very smart animals. They can escape from just about anywhere. My brother's husky, whose name is Hershey, has escaped at least five different times, and it's always from a different place. They are also very furry animals and they shed a lot! They are great family dogs and love to be around adults and children. They also love to play and are very active and seem to never run out of energy. One of the downsides to this is if you live in an apartment building or small house, your husky doesn't have much room to play, so it's best to take them out and let them run or play at a park.

Huskies are originally from Siberia, a part of northern Asia, and were originally bred to be sled dogs and to help haul large loads for hunters in the area. They were and still are one of the most successful sled dog breeds in the world. They are very strong and can run long distances without getting tired. One famous story about their abilities to run long distances was the Serum Run of 1925.

Nome, Alaska was having a diphtheria outbreak and didn't have enough medicine. But the nearest town that had any medicine was Anchorage, which was 1,000 miles away. They had a train that brought the medicine to within 660 miles of Nome, but there was no other way to get the medicine to Nome. So a group of 20 drivers and 100 dogs set out on a mail route through the wilderness in a blizzard to retrieve the medicine. This trail usually took 25 days to complete, but these dogs did it in 6.

Almost all of these dogs were Siberian Huskies. While there were many dogs who helped bring the medicine to Nome, the most famous was a dog named Balto. He was the lead dog on the last sled in the relay to bring the medicine in. He saved his team from getting lost by sniffing out the right trail to follow in a blizzard! Today there is a statue of Balto in Central Park.

This great feat of getting medicine over such a long distance in the snow began a traditional race known as the Iditarod. It is still run every year in Alaska. And the dogs that run it are huskies because of their strength and reputation for being hardworking animals.

Siberian Huskies can also be able to talk. Mishka the talking husky is one a lot of people know. Mishka is all over Facebook and the Internet. Mishka mimics what her owners say to her. She can say "I love you," "I'm hungry," and "I want potatoes." That is only a little bit of what Mishka can say. Mishka can say all kinds of words.

Laika and Mishka can talk to each other, and you will be able to understand them. Mishka is older than Laika, and they like to play together. They really enjoyed the Blizzard of 2016 and playing in the snow. They have become famous over the internet on YouTube and Facebook.

Siberian Huskies are great dogs. They can be fun pets and are very loyal. Siberian Huskies are very smart and can be trained to do just about anything. They are mischievous and can be escape artists, so you have to watch them carefully. Having a Siberian Husky is a lot of fun.

Middle School Essay

Cheyenne Pine is an eighth grade student at Midway Middle School.

Self-Harm

Self-harm is a dangerous way that people cope with their problems. Everyone at some point in their life goes through something tragic, some people use self-harm as a way to escape. Self-harm comes in many forms: cutting, hitting, or punching yourself, sometimes even drugs or alcohol is considered self-harm. I can say for myself that self-harm is as addicting as smoking or drinking. Once you start, there is no escaping it.

Most people who self-harm are teenagers. They don't always know how to cope with their problems, such as bullying or personal problems, they self-harm to feel better. There are many dangerous effects that come from self-harm. Many teens have died from self-harm or been hospitalized. There are better ways to cope with your problems than self-harm.

What is self-harm? Self-harm is a dangerous way that teens use to "escape" their problems. Self-harm comes in many different forms. A person can cut themselves, hit, punch, or kick themselves, sometimes even drugs or alcohol is considered self-harm. Anything that causes yourself harm, hence the name, "self-harm," is considered self-harm. Most teens who harm themselves think it's okay; they need to know that it's really not.

When teens start harming themselves, it becomes very addicting. You start to harm yourself and forget about all your problems. You don't realize that this has become a routine. Most teens don't realize how addicting it is. They don't realize that once they start, there is no going back. Not only is it addicting, but there are consequences from self-harm. Teens have managed to kill themselves or put themselves in the hospital. Even if you're lucky and don't end up in the hospital, you will still have scars. When teens harm themselves, they don't think of future consequences. We all know that summer is when you wear shorts and t-shirts, but teens who harm themselves usually don't because of scaring. You don't realize that you'll have those scars forever, and sometimes those scars can cause bullying and make you feel embarrassed. Teens don't realize the serious consequences that come from self-harm.

Self-harm is something very dangerous. Most teens use self-harm as a way to "escape," not realizing, that self-harm is not helping them any, but only harming them. Most teens have to be pushed to the edge before they start harming themselves. Self-harm could be caused from a tragic event, depression, or bullying. Sometimes, teens will even do it for attention. Self-harm has serious effects. Many teens have killed themselves, even if they weren't trying to. Others have been seriously injured and hospitalized. Some teens get lucky and have never been in the hospital before, but it's a rarity. Even if you're in that few percent that doesn't go to the hospital, your parents won't be too happy either. Whether they're sad or mad, they won't be happy with you at all. Most teens think that their parents won't understand, but you'd be surprised. I thought my parents wouldn't care, but it turns out they really did. Instead of harming yourself, talk to your parents or a trusted friend.

Self-harm is a dangerous way people cope with their problems. Almost everyone goes through something tragic in their life at some point. Only some people use self-harm as a way to escape the issues in their life. Self-harm can come in multiple different ways. These ways include: cutting, hitting, or punching yourself, sometimes even alcohol or drug abuse. Self-harm is something that becomes very addicting. Once you start, you can't stop. The majority of people who self-harm are teenagers. Teens can start harming themselves for many reasons. These reasons include: depression, bullying, and personal problems. Teens like to use self-harm to make themselves feel better. Teens think that if they use self-harm, they will be able to escape their problems. Only the issue is teens don't seem to realize that what they are doing to themselves isn't helping them escape their problems at all. In fact, it's only making it worse.

Teens need to understand that there are better ways to cope with their problems rather than harming themselves. Some of these ways include simple things like talking to an adult or your parents. Even talking to a trusted friend will help you out. You need to feel confident about talking to someone; once you become confident then find a well trusted adult or friend and let it out. If you know this person cares about you, then it should be easier to tell them. Although it can seem hard as well because you might think that they don't care or they don't understand. Surprisingly, almost anyone that you trust will find some way to help you. Instead of harming yourself, talk to someone you trust. This will make you feel a lot better than harming yourself will.

Middle School Essay

Ben Poczobut is an eighth grade student at Midway Middle School.

The History of Lacrosse

The history of lacrosse might be more than you think. Did you know that lacrosse was first played by Native Americans? It originates from the East Coast of North America. It was played by tribes including the Oneida, Onondaga, Mohawk, and Seneca tribes. Europeans first discovered lacrosse around 1630. The earliest game was in the 1500's.

Evolution of lacrosse has changed a lot since the first Native Americans played. The early Native American game included many players, upwards of 5000. The games started by throwing a small wooden ball into the air as a swarm of people chased to get it. The goal was a tall wooden post with different spots marked on it. The first line was about chest level. The next was higher than arm reach and the third was even higher. If you hit the first mark or above you scored one point; the second, two points; and the third, three points. The stick was about two and half feet long that had a large net on the end that held the ball.

Men mostly played but in some versions women did play. When women played, they mostly did not use sticks, but used their hands. Also men who were too rough with the women were penalized or thrown out of the game. When women did not play, they mostly supplied refreshments to the men. The Medicine Men acted as coaches to the game. Young men played the game and women, old men, and children watched the games.

The first rules of lacrosse weren't very strict mostly because lacrosse was considered a war game. But there were some, including the goal which had to be a certain height, the markings had to be correct, and usually there was a picture of a certain bird at the top. Also, there were restrictions on who played lacrosse. Only young strong men who could fight in battle could play in the normal game, although there were other games designated to men and women.

Traditional lacrosse games were major events. Playing time was from sunup to sundown and could last several days. The goals could be as close as five hundred yards apart to as far as six miles apart, depending on the how many people were playing the games. The night before the game players would decorate their bodies and sticks with paint and other materials. The Medicine Man performed rituals to prepare the players and their sticks before the game. On the day of the game, the two teams would walk to the field. When they got to the field, the Shaman gave a strategic pep talk. Before the game, players were made to place a wager on the game. Items including knives, trinkets, even horses, children, and wives would be at stake. When the game was over, a feast for the players was held.

Early lacrosse balls were made out of wood, deer skin, or rocks. The first lacrosse sticks were essentially giant wooden spears that elevated to more of a circle that was filled with deer sinew netting. The sticks were bent into shape with steaming.

Today, lacrosse is nothing like what the Native Americans played. Present day lacrosse includes stick sizes depending on the position played, chest pads, helmets, gloves, elbow pads, and cleats. Lacrosse sticks can range from seventy to seventy-two inches long and are made of aluminum shaft with a plastic head and cotton strings for the net. The lacrosse ball is made of a solid rubber ball that is usually white in color. Midfielders need to be fast with a lot of stamina. Defensemen need to be powerful and agile. The goalie needs to be fast in a six by six-foot area. The goalie also has to be one of the toughest on the team because he/she gets up to 100 miles per hour shots toward them.

Present day lacrosse rules are much stricter than what the traditional lacrosse was. In lacrosse, you have to wear a helmet, chest pads, gloves, and elbow pads. Things that aren't allowed include: slashing, which is the hitting with the stick to the helmet or shoulders; tripping, which is tripping your opponent; crease violation, which is stepping within the crease that is around the goal; unnecessary roughness and unsportsmanlike conduct, all of which are as they sound; and off sides, which includes having more than six players on one side of the field at any time, not including the goalie. The lacrosse field is one hundred ten yards in length by sixty yards in width. Also out of bound is the ball going out of the one hundred ten by sixty-yard field.

Lacrosse is the fastest growing sport in America. Lacrosse is the fastest sport on two feet. The first women's lacrosse game was played in Scotland in 1890. In the summer of 1763, lacrosse was played by two tribes to distract British soldiers in order to recapture fort Michilioncikica.

Middle School Essay

Connor Quigley is an eighth grade student at Midway Middle School.

Football

Football is one of the most popular American sports. It is a sport first played in the 1800s. Football is a sport that involves pads for protection. In football, the goal is to get to the other team's goal and end up with more points. In football, a ball encased in pigskin is used to score. In this game, if the ball touches the ground, it is dead in most cases. Only in one case is it not dead when it is behind the line of scrimmage. The line is what yard line the ball is on. You have four downs or times the whistle is blown for signaling the ball is down. Football was first played in America.

Football's equipment has changed much over time. The padding in them has softened, but it also has become more absorbent. People have gotten injuries due to faulty equipment. Injuries to the head are called concussions. Concussions are more serious than most other types of injuries. This is because concussions can cause brain damage. All injuries in this game are taken very seriously because every injury can be serious, but concussions are taken very seriously. This game has gradually increased the protection for its players. The helmets became more absorbent to take impact. The shoulder pads became more absorbent. The leg padding became thicker and much stronger and less likely to crack. This game is so rough that people can even be knocked unconscious. Believe it or not, bones can be broken during this game.

Not everyone plays in the same leagues. There are separate leagues of football. Two of these leagues are college and the NFL. In college, only people attending that college can play on that team. NFL and college are sort of related. Players from college go up for draft after their last year in college, and the NFL picks the ones they want. In college, you are limited to how many years you can play. In the NFL, though, you are not limited on how old you can play to. In the NFL you don't have to stay on the same team your whole career. You can transfer to another team if you want. In the college, it just matters what college you are attending. Also, in the NFL you can get paid up to 1.2 million dollars a year. In college though, you do not get paid because you are attending the college and paying that school.

There isn't just one type of football either. There are multiple variants of the sport. There is the regular, then there is flag and many more. In flag football, there is a little change in rules. In this variant, there is no tackling. There is simply a flag attached to the players. To get them down you have to remove the flag from its resting position on the player. One more change, they have no pads on their legs because they are not getting hit in the legs. They do keep helmets and shoulder pads though. Why they do that is beyond me. In flag football basically all the same rules apply except there is barely any physical contact because the players are not fully padded. Therefore they are not fully protected from hits that would happen in regular football. Fumbles and everything else like passing are the same. When you drop a pass in flag football it is also an incomplete.

When you do something against the rules, it is called a penalty. When you get a penalty, your team gives the other team yards. When a penalty is called, you have to surrender a certain number of yards based on how serious the foul was. There are many different reasons why penalties are called. Some are because of un-sportsmen-like conduct. This is also known as bragging or excessive celebration. Some are because you have violated the line of scrimmage. This is known as off-sides. Most penalties called are not for serious reasons like fights or anything violent. Penalties exist in all types or variants of football. When penalties are called, it causes the other team to gain or lose yards. If it is an offensive penalty, like holding, then the offense is penalized. If a defensive penalty is called, like off-sides, then it penalizes the defense.

American football was first played in the 1800s. It was formed by a rugby player. When formed, it had rules made. The teams had eleven men each. This was to make sure each team had an even chance to win the game. Many different variants were made of this game. Flag football is one example different from the original version. When someone does something wrong, a penalty is called. This causes the penalized team to lose yards or give a better position to the other team which might cause them to lose the game. These are the reason I love football. It is a fun game in my opinion. This is also why I enjoy watching it.

Middle School Essay

Savanna Rayburn is an eighth grade student at Midway Middle School.

Animal Cruelty

Animal cruelty is an ever-growing problem that affects a large number of the Earth's population of animals. In fact, every day around the world there is an animal that is being abused. The people who abuse and neglect these animals do any kind of physical or emotional harm to the animal itself to cause the animal the most hurt they possibly can. Many animal abuse cases do not end well at all, but there are many that end very good for the animal's wellbeing. Animals are mistreated and misunderstood every day, and there are many people who try to help animals, such as the teams called, "Peta," "ASPCA," and the "Humane Society" helps animals every day all around the world. These teams go out every day to help end this situation. Neglecting and abusing an animal could cause an animal to be violent with others, untrusting toward other animals or people, or be scared of everything. In fact, in America alone, there are almost one to two-thousand animals abused and neglected every day. These animal support teams want to lower this number to just zero.

In an animal abuse or a neglect case, the animal that has been abused or neglected could have a very difficult time finding a foster or forever home. This reason is because the many terrible situations that the animal has been through could cause the animal to be very untrusting of people. Animal abuse is a very serious problem around the world that affects each and every animal and individual in it. All anti-cruelty laws do exist in all of the U.S. states and territories to prohibit any kind of unnecessary killing, mutilating, torturing, beating, neglecting, or abandoning animals.

An animal cruelty case is investigated by a local humane society, SPCA, or a local police department. When the investigation uncovers enough evidence to convict an individual, charges may be filed by the local district or state's attorney. Even though there are many kinds of animal abuse cases, two abuse cases particularly troubled me deeply. They were the killing of a Fox- Terrier named "Peanut" and the dragging of a small pit-bull puppy named "Trooper." They both are terribly sad tales that involve these small pups.

Here are Peanut's and Trooper's stories: In the year of 2008, a pair of men kidnapped a fox terrier puppy named Peanut from his home, took him to a park behind some rodeo grounds, and recorded themselves slashing him with a knife and garden shears, amputating two of his legs and severing his nose, before finally decapitating him. One of the men allegedly had a "falling out" with Peanut's female owner and tortured the dog as an act of revenge. It was described as "the worst case of animal cruelty in Australian history."

Early in the year of 2012, a male pit bull puppy named Trooper had his leash attached to the back of a pickup truck and was dragged for nearly a mile. According to a director of a local Humane Society, "He could barely sit up on his own, and he was extremely weak from blood loss, having gone through what he went through." Trooper survived and was put up for adoption.

There are many different cases that have a sadder ending than others, but there are many others that have, thankfully, a happy ending for the animal. One of these cases is the case of the young pup, Tuffy, that was covered in a boiling tub of water, and then tossed from a fourth-story balcony because of chewing his owner's phone. His body was covered in so many blisters that he couldn't even close his eyes to rest, but after months and months of recovering, and a little TLC, Tuffy pulled through.

Animal cruelty is a problem that many pets face every day, and many people try to end forever. Many stories inspire people to help stop animal abuse forever. The many reasons why some breeds of animals are abused and neglected such as because of their history. Two examples of this are the American pit bull and the Doberman dog breeds. This is because of the history of the fights between two or more dogs, called "Dog-fighting." Dog fighting dates back to around 241 A.D. and is a felony offense in all 50 states, and it is the program in which two dogs are thrown into one small dog pen or some type of cage and then forced to fight each other. Their fights can last just a few minutes or even several hours. Both of the dogs or animals may suffer injuries such as puncture wounds, lacerations, blood loss, crushing injuries, and even broken bones. Many people, who try to stop these fights are not successful, but there are many who are successful. "Let's put a paw in stopping animal abuse."

The difference that we make today can impact our tomorrow in stopping animal abuse forever. We have not yet successfully ended animal abuse, but we will keep trying until we are successful. Animal abuse affects everyone involved, from the animals, to the owners, to the rescuers. Animals are misunderstood and mistreated on a daily basis; together we can put this to a complete stop. Together we can make a difference in stopping animal abuse. "If these animals never gave up, we can't give up either."

Middle School Essay

Emilee Schaefer is a seventh grade student who is homeschooled.

A Man's Best Friend

I know we have all heard the phrase "dogs are a man's best friend." Today I want to prove this correct. We're going to be talking about how dogs encourage people to put their mistakes in the past, how they help you if you are scared, can even help with police and blind people, how they relieve you of stress, help stop or combat depression and loneliness, that they love you the way you are, help to keep you healthy, and understand your emotions.

Being human, we all make mistakes. Friends, even who we call our best friends, may take our mistakes and use them against us to make us look bad to hurt us. Dogs, on the other hand, have a short term memory. So no matter how many mistakes you make, they'll forget in a few minutes and go back to being your best friend.

Ever been home alone and that package delivery dude rings the doorbell and bangs on the door but you wouldn't dare open it? Don't worry! In a matter of just a few seconds, your dog is acting as your protector, barking away at whoever it is at the door. He completely scares away that person! Police stations even have dogs as canine officers. They help find drugs and deal with mean people. Some dogs are therapeutic and are working dogs to help blind people get around safely.

Have you ever had a big test and you're feeling really stressed? Go hang out with your little pal for a few minutes. It is a proven fact that when you're stressed, you should pet a puppy or kitten, and it will relieve your stress. Even at some colleges, they have puppy and kitten rooms during students' finals week so that stressed-out students can spend some enjoyable time petting puppies and kittens. Pretty neat, isn't it?

Dogs also come in and help with depression and loneliness. I have heard it's also a proven fact that suicide is less common for people who own pets. Life can get really depressing sometimes, can't it? You may go through break-ups, friends may hurt you, and people at school might even make fun of you. What do I do when I'm down, you ask? Well, I find my little pet Dachshund, Dexter, and wrap him in my arms. You're never lonely when you have a dog! Wherever you go, they want to be right there with you. Many older people have pets to keep them company and keep away the loneliness.

Your dog doesn't judge you, no matter what kind of clothes you wear, no matter if you're rich or poor, he loves you just the way you are. Are you coming home from work looking and feeling exhausted? A person might judge you for that, but your dog doesn't care, he's just glad his best friend is home.

Your dog is also great for keeping you healthy and in good shape. Dog owners have lots of benefits. One benefit is dog owners have lower cholesterol and they also have fewer heart attacks. This basically means that dog owners have less medical problems than persons without a dog. Your dog also keeps you up and active. They encourage you to exercise more by begging for a walk and wanting to play.

Dogs understand your emotions. They can tell by the tone of your voice and how you act if you are upset. They try to tell you they care by their little whimpers and big puppy eyes they give you. They stare at you to make sure you see that they care.

I hope that by reading this, you have come to the realization that the phrase "dogs are a man's best friend" is true. We are blessed that God gave us these wonderful creatures to be our companions, friends, and even co-workers. Go pet a dog today!

Middle School Essay

Stephen Wishnia is an eighth grade student at Midway Middle School.

Is your faith under attack?

Should people die for what they believe? The answer is most definitely not! We should not be judged for what we believe teach or preach or say about what we believe. There are many religious groups that want to spread only their belief, which is very wrong! Groups like ISIS and other extremist groups would go as far as killing a person that may be hindering their religious beliefs or the spreading of their belief. We need to take a stand against these religious bullies and stop the discrimination of other religions. There are a few countries that are being forced to join the extremist religion, either by threat or by force.

In a magazine called the "Voice of the Martyrs," it describes a man walking down an alleyway when suddenly he is confronted by a mob of extremists. They asked him, "Will you join us or will you die?" The man stated that he will not join the group and upon saying that, the man was instantly killed. There a few people who are willing to give their life for what they believe, like this man did. There are also some that fear for their lives. In the same magazine, it shares a story about a woman confronted by a mob and asked her the same question, "Will you join us or will you die?" The woman answered yes, and no one has heard from her since that day. Some people are less courageous than others.

Let's focus for a while on the main extremist group in the world, ISIS! ISIS has grown to be the biggest terror group in the world and is expanding its territory every day. The religion of that group is Muslim, the biggest and fastest growing religion in the world today. Muslims believe that they have to expand their religion and be obedient to the orders of "Allah," the God figure of the Muslim religion, to go to Heaven. They supposedly get these orders from their most holy book, the "Koran." The book states that you have to spread the religion in order to go to Heaven, even if it means that you have to kill somebody in order to perform the task that "Allah" gives you. Muslim extremists also think that they are doing absolutely nothing wrong! If the Koran says to do something, then they are going to do what it says without complaining. We need to show ISIS that what they are doing is wrong and stop their acts of violence.

Unfortunately, they probably will not listen to what we have to say, but all we can do is try. But this does not mean that all Muslims are bad people; in fact, we have more peaceful Muslims in America than we do extremist Muslims. Most Muslims live peacefully with Americans and are tolerant of other religions in America. So we should not think of Muslims as bad people. As a matter of fact, we should not treat any other religion that is not our own disrespectfully! It goes back all the way to kindergarten: Treat others as you want to be treated. That is what America really needs to emphasize.

It's not always religious groups that are discriminating against other religious groups. There are some people who are biased when it comes to religions and often talk about how bad the other religions are or how that one is a joke. America was established on religious tolerance, peace, and tranquility; that does not sound like religious tolerance to me! America needs to go back to the ways that our forefathers established. I know that this may seem like a controversial and a confrontational message, but like I said, most Muslims in America are happy to live in a country that offers them so many freedoms. They are tolerant of other religions.

On September 11, 2001, there were Muslim radicals from the Middle East who crashed planes into the World Trade Centers, and from that we declared war on the Muslim radicals and have been fighting them ever since then! Even though they did such a horrible thing, we should not look at all Muslims that way. As some people would say, they were only following their religion. We should look beyond that, show them that they are wrong for what they believe, such as hurting people in order to go to Heaven. Show them that there is a better way than to kill and destroy innocent lives. We all have heard the phrase, "lives matter," so let us do more to show people that they really do matter!

In conclusion, there are many extremist religious groups that want to spread their religion and will stop at nothing to get it done. They will go as far as killing someone that might be hindering their work. We need to show those extremists that they are doing wrong and stop all the religious blood that is being shed by these groups of extremists who think they are doing absolutely nothing wrong! They believe that they will go to Heaven if they follow the God of the Muslims, who supposedly gives his orders from their most holy book, the Koran. Still, we should not bash somebody or some group just because we do not agree with their religion. But rather reason with them. Treat others as you want to be treated is a phrase that is tossed around like a hot potato and nobody knows what to do with it. We as Americans should know how to use this phrase. The world is under attack, in a religious war; you may not see it with the naked eye, but the world is torn apart spiritually. We must work together to put the world back together. So let us take a stand against these groups and show them that there is a better way, the way of peace!

Acknowledgements

The Roane County Student Writing Contest has been generously supported by students, parents, school teachers and administrators, volunteers, and members of the Roane Writers Group. This anthology is funded by an Arts Builds Communities grant from the Tennessee Arts Commission.

Special thanks to:

Arts Council of Roane County

Gary Aytes, Director of Roane County Schools

Brooks Benjamin

Cliff Lynch Family

Jasmine DeGroot

Carolyn Granger – Roane County Commissioner

Sharon Higa

Greg Johnson – Entertainer at *johnsonville@aol.com*

Kingston Public Library

Larry and Sandra Gabbard

Phyllis Jackson

Dr. Timothy Joseph

Allen Lutz, Director of Education Matters Volunteers

Kat Moore

Roane Alliance

Robin Haase

Roane County Chamber of Commerce

Roane State Community College

Roane Writers Group

Tennessee Arts Commission

Ken Yager, Tennessee State Senator

What Can I Do To Help?

So you're a supporter of writing? Of literacy in schools? Of getting children to write more and better? Are you wondering how you can help with this writing contest? Help in the form of time, resources, and money is always needed.

All monetary donations can be made by check to the "Roane Writers Group" and write in the memo field "Writing Contest Awards." Checks may be delivered to:

>Citizens National Bank
>202 N. Kentucky St.
>Kingston, Tennessee 37763

or mailed to

>Citizens National Bank
>P.O. Box 545
>Kingston, Tennessee 37763-0545

The public can obtain copies of the anthology at the Citizen's National Bank of Kingston, Kingston Public Library and The Roane Alliance for a donation of ten dollars or more per copy. These donations will go toward funding the awards program for the fall 2016 school year.

Roane Writers Group is a member of the Arts Council of Roane County, a 501(c)3 non-profit organization, and The Roane County Chamber of Commerce.

All inquiries can be directed to B.J. Gillum by phone at 865-354-8658 or by e-mail at bjgillum@comcast.net.
Thank you for your support of the Roane Writers Group!

Special Thanks to Our Supporting Advertisers

We wish to express our special thanks to the individuals and organizations on the following pages that support the Roane Writers Group with their financial support.

Their support provides the prizes and continuing education scholarships that go to our winning student authors. Without their support the prizes and scholarships would not be possible.

Thank you!

Our mission is to strive to create an environment & unified voice that promotes:
Job creation
Economic development
Enhanced quality of life
Education & workforce development

Roane ECD
roanealliance.org

Development of a well-trained workforce to meet current and emerging job requirements of

Roane Tourism
roanetourism.com

Continuing growth of business and tourism, and promotion

Roane Chamber
roanechamber.com

Support of both existing and new businesses and industries by enhancing and promoting the

Education Matters
educationmatters2roane.com

Educational and workforce development programs that influence collaborations to successfully motivate our citizens to

Retire Roane
retireroane.com

Establishing Roane County as the regional destination to live, work, play and visit.

Unified Drive. United Force.

1209 N. Kentucky St, Kingston ♦ 865.376.2093 ♦ roanealliance.org

Congratulations to the Roane Writers Group for another year of creative encouragement and service to our student writers and community!

Thank you!

Ken Yager
Tennessee State Senator
District 12

Roane County Recycling Center

215 White Pine Road
Harriman, TN 37748
865-590-7779
Ralph Stewart, Director

Recycled Materials Accepted:
Used Motor Oil and Antifreeze
Plastic (Milk Jugs, Drink Bottles, Detergent Bottles)
Cardboard
Mixed Paper
Scrap Metal
Aluminum
Batteries

 The ACRC is dedicated to enriching cultural life within Roane County through programs and partnerships that celebrate artistic excellence, cultivate artistic opportunities, & promote educational activities.

We welcome new members to join us—attend meetings, help plan events, or participate in whatever way you are comfortable. If you are interested or would like to join, visit our website, or email us and we will send you information on becoming a member.

We meet at the Roane Central Utility Building, 2727 Roane State Highway, Harriman, TN 37748 on the third Tuesday of each month at 6:30 p.m.

Photo by Wayne Setzer

For more information, visit http://artscouncilrc.com
Like us on Facebook
Email: artscouncilofroanecounty@gmail.com

Congratulations to the Roane Writers Group for another year of exceptional community service!

RON WOODY, CPA, CGFM, CSBA
ROANE COUNTY EXECUTIVE
ron.woody@roanecountytn.gov
www.roanecountytn.gov

200 East Race Street, Suite #1
Post Office Box 643
Kingston, Tennessee 37763
Phone 865-376-5578 • Fax 865-717-4215

Congratulations from

Kingston, Roane County, Tennessee

Made in the USA
Charleston, SC
20 May 2016